Praise for Camping with K

"*What is worthy of my finitude?* There's a term mountain bikers use: *dropping in.* It means you're entering a steep, technical trail. It's time to trust your training, conditioning, and preparation. Everything contracts to muscle memory, instinct, and awareness—pure presence in the moment. But only if you commit, *really* commit. J. Aaron Simmons calls us to live like that. Do the work of inquiry and examination, ask the hard questions, but not as an intellectual exercise or as careerists. Instead, he would have us undertake the care of the self in order to commit and be present in our finitude: to know the love of family and friends, the beauty of nature, and the presence of the transcendent. *The mountains are calling and I must go*, runs the saying. Well, your *life* is calling and you must go. Take this book with you for the journey."

　　–Travis E. Ables, Theologian, Mountain Biker and Bikepacker

"Aaron Simmons treats his readers to a lively discussion of philosophical heavyweights, contemporary music, personal recollections and hard-won wisdom, all the while guiding and goading us to think about how we live our lives. Quick-witted, endlessly inventive and invigorating, Simmons sets a brisk pace in a text that is at once an excellent introduction to philosophical discourse, a free-wheeling chronicle of a scholar's life, and a model of effective teaching, with fresh takes on the contributions of thinkers from Aristotle to Nietzsche, from Judith Butler to Jean Chrétien. Most remarkable, perhaps, is Simmons's disarming gift for alternating between light-hearted banter, pointed social critique and earnest Kierkegaardian exhortation. A trip to the mountains imminently worth taking."

　　–Vanessa Rumble, Philosopher, Hiker

"This Thoreau-like reflection could be called "Mountain Biking with Kierkegaard." If you take the ride and you should, you will imbibe lessons like the connection between avoiding trees on your mountain bike and avoiding becoming a crowd person. Some of the deepest philosophical probes are on humility, hospitality, and gratitude, but all the philosophical points are artfully connected with embodied experience."

–**Gordon Marino**, Philosopher, Boxer, Author
of *The Existentialist's Survival Guide*

"Aaron Simmons has given us a great gift in this beautifully written, down-to-earth, exploration of the big questions of faith, ethics, vulnerability, and resilience. We feel the cold of a late autumn evening, the warmth of a cocoa cup by the campfire as thoughtfulness and connection are revived as real possibilities. Philosophical questions leave the halls of academic conferences and enter flesh and blood. We are reminded that philosophy allows us to pierce the veil of cultural expectation and dive into the struggle and joy of life itself. His years at work in the fields of continental philosophy merge with his devotion to camping and fishing to produce profound reflections on living a life of faithfulness and meaning on and off the trails of our beautiful earthly home."

–**Wendy Farley**, Theologian, Hiker, Author of *Beguiled by Beauty*

"In *Camping with Kierkegaard*, Aaron Simmons makes philosophy accessible and demonstrates how much wisdom philosophers like Kierkegaard have to teach us today. In an age of hurry, consumerism, and binary thinking with over simplistic answers, Aaron invites the reader to ponder what exactly is worthy of our time as finite beings, or put another way: "What is worthy of our finitude?" Self-aware, Aaron doesn't expect us to live life like he does, but instead to find our own way to be present in the moment with our loved ones, experiencing the beauty and fullness that life has to offer here and now."

–**Tim Whitaker**, Creator of "The New
Evangelicals" Podcast, Drummer

"In a narrative that an outdoor enthusiast will enjoy via accessibility and wit, Simmons shares the hard-earned insights of the big thinkers of philosophy for a well-reasoned account of why we should live the examined life and suggestions about how we can live it well. This book invites us to strive for a better quality of life for ourselves that's certain to extend to others."

–Dustin Cook, Entrepreneur, Skydiver, Mountain Biker

"Simmons claims that he "marks his life by rivers." As an angler, I do as well. Simmons's book, *Camping with Kierkegaard*, shows that faith and hope may be best found on a trout stream (or a mountain bike trail or hiking path) and are the pact every angler signs when they step into the water. Faith and hope exist in the next cast, the changing of a fly pattern, and the unknown of what's beyond that bend of the river up ahead. They are found in the simple act of becoming the thing you already are."

–David N. McIlvaney, Writer, Outdoorsman, Huckleberry

Wɪsᴅᴏᴍ/Wᴏʀᴋ
Published by Wisdom Work
TomVMorris.com

©2023 by Aaron Simmons
Cover concept by Waylon Bigsby

ISBN: 979-8-9889606-0-7
Subjects: Philosophy

Printed in the United States of America

CAMPING WITH KIERKEGAARD

Faithfulness as a Way of Life

J. Aaron Simmons

For Atticus

Table of Contents

I cannot write it here in the city; so I must take a journey.
–Kierkegaard August 27, 1844[1]

Hope springs from that which is right in front of us,
which surprises us, and seems to work.
–Anne Lamott (2018, p. 181)

---

1   As cited in the "Historical Introduction" to (Kierkegaard 1988, ix).

Foreword

Aaron Simmons is a contemporary version of Thoreau, but friendlier and, honestly, a much better philosopher than that particular Sage of Concord and its vast woodland environment. He's a rock music drummer, a mountain biker, a fisherman, a hiker and camper and a man who has an unerring instinct for what's important, both in the world and in our lives. His voice is one we deeply need in our time. In this long-awaited book, he steps outside the academy where he's had major intellectual success for many years and speaks to all of us about some of the things that matter most in our lives. He talks about how we can get our bearings and find our philosophical revelations outside, in nature, as the most effective laboratory and classroom of all. He invites us to join him as he hikes and bikes and wades in the water and casts his lures and thoughts, then pitches camp to reflect on what he's learned along the way. You'll be spellbound by the fireside chats.

My favorite professor at Yale long ago, in an uncharacteristically vulnerable and candid moment, once told my class of graduate students and divinity school scholars that he'd had some of his greatest philosophical experiences in nature, and in particular while lying in a canoe floating silently on a placid lake under clear skies and bright

i

stars on summer nights in Minnesota. He described to us how he had experienced the wonders of the cosmos, the unavoidable mysteries of existence, and a sense of enveloping wisdom that led him into deep thinking, engaged teaching, and committed writing with a voice nowhere else to be found. He influenced generations of Yale students and through them countless other people, young and old, for a great many decades and perhaps endlessly into the future. Such is the power of nature's influence for an open heart and mind.

An earlier favorite professor at the University of North Carolina, where I was fortunate to be a Morehead Scholar, now the Morehead-Cain, years before I arrived at Yale, had one day memorably said to our class of hundreds of undergraduates that "Atheism is an urban phenomenon." He went on to explain that those who live in cities can easily think their bread simply comes from the baker, their meat from the butcher, their vegetables just from the corner grocery store. They live in a humanly constructed environment cut off from nature, and the towers of Babel around them can easily block out the light of the sun, the moon, and the stars. The asphalt and concrete will not allow the earth to speak, or even deeper sources to communicate their truths. And yet historically, those who live in nature, closer to the elementary forces, tend to see things differently and perhaps more clearly, while hearing quite another song than the cacophony of noise and smog that a humanly constructed context will allow.

Aaron Simmons takes us back into the nature that first gave us life and can give it to us again anew, traveling along mountain bike trails, beside riverbeds, and into waters where the fish await us with their whispered secrets. He invites us to camp, commune, and converse with him, along with other great minds like Søren Kierkegaard, a favorite of my old Yale professor, and he includes many others as well. He pulls back the curtains of our carefully contrived civilization and introduces us to the fundamentals of our condition here on earth. He insists that we decide what to make of our finitude and that we base our choices on truth and faithfulness, as well as real wisdom.

If you've ever seen up close the famous statue that represents philosophy, August Rodin's "Thinker," you may have noticed that he's a very muscular individual. He's a man of action as well as of deep thought. And that's the right combination. Action without thought and thought without action may equally miss the mark. But it's the two together that can be magical in their results. And they come together in this book.

Aaron's a husband and a father, a teacher, and a thinker. He's an active man fully engaged in the diverse challenges of life. He works with university students and with businesspeople from all walks of life. He shares questions and answers with top scholars and ordinary folks, who inevitably turn out to be not so ordinary at all. And it's from this widely diverse cauldron of engagement and its concurrent mix of experiences that some of his best insights arise. But they tend to bubble up into consciousness when he's out in the wild on a new adventure.

Aaron is a quintessential scholar, highly respected and at the pinnacle of the profession. He's the sort of rare faculty member that universities love and prize and that the rest of us find too seldom in the world today. He has introduced me to many insights from a variety of great thinkers in the past that I would most likely have missed on my own. I love to read everything he writes, as well as to see his short and high impact videos on social media. Google him and follow him. Stay in conversation with him. But you will get some of the best and most personal wisdom right here in this book. He's camping with Kierkegaard and we're tagging along with both of them in these pages for their revelations about life and love and wisdom. A number of other campers also show up, and they all have great and important things to say. There are new perspectives here that you can't likely find anywhere else. And you will benefit, as I have, from their depth and practicality, a combination rarely to be found in our time.

So, check over your mountain bike. Make sure everything's in good shape for a wild ride. Lace up your boots well. And see to it that you have your fishing gear all ready for action when you get close to the stream. Aaron has packed up a really nice tent that he knows how to put up fast. He's got some great food prepared for the trail. And the setting will be great. You're in for a treat. I just wish old Thoreau could have come along. He would have become a major fan of this book and its author, just as I am.

–Tom Morris

Preface
Join me by the Campfire

There is something different about the shadows that a campfire casts. Unlike the shadows on the sidewalk during the midst of the day, campfire shadows don't stay still. They dance unpredictably. They are alive.

As I sit here by the fire, with my tent behind me, and my truck in front of me (with fishing rods in the bed and mountain bike attached to the rack), I am where I want to be. While my shadow dances, I am still. Peace is my companion. Joy is my friend.

The hot chocolate that I made on my camp stove warms my hands even as the brisk autumn air chills my cheeks. Here by the fire, this paradox of hot and cold doesn't meld into a mushy compromise, but instead reminds me that life is always a matter of extremes: birth and death, joy and despair, vice and virtue, risk and reward. Figuring out how to navigate those extremes is what life requires. Just as the wood won't burn without oxygen, too much wind and the fire becomes too dangerous to start. Life is like that. Somehow we have to find ways to get the fire started without allowing it to burn down the forest around us.

There are two squirrels in a tree just a few yards away. Perhaps they have come near to see if there is some food that has been carelessly dropped by the unaware camper? Maybe they also seek the warmth of the fire? Or could it be that they are simply out for an evening date among the trees?

In the distance I can hear a small waterfall on the river that runs near my campsite. It is staggering to me that folks pay a lot of money for apps that will play the sounds of a river to help them sleep, but those same people are often resistant to going to the mountains in order to spend time near rivers.

For my part, I largely mark my life by rivers.

There is a particular spot on a river in Gatlinburg, TN where I remember vividly sitting while I was in high school. Watching the water play over the rocks I thought about what I hoped my life would look like. There is another spot by the Hiwassee River in Reliance, TN where I asked my wife to marry me. On a river in Dupont State Forest outside Hendersonville, NC I once caught the biggest brown trout of my life and yet it slipped out of my hands before my dad could get a picture. Seriously. I have a picture of simply my empty hands, but no trout. That same river is one that I often jump into in order to cool off after a long mountain bike ride in the summer heat. For what it is worth, it is also the river where several scenes from the amazingly beautiful film, *The Last of the Mohicans*, were shot.

It is interesting to me that so many philosophers have used rivers and mountains to make significant points about the meaning and purpose of human existence. I think that they were definitely on to something.

I admit that my mind keeps jumping to tomorrow when I will get the bike out on the trails in Pisgah National Forest and then in the afternoon hit the Davidson River, or maybe the North Mills River depending on what the water levels are like, and see if I can get a few trout. But, and this is crucial, *that* anticipation is not the cause of the joy *now*. The campfire, the stars, the slight breeze, the taste of the hot chocolate, and the dancing shadows are, in themselves, enough.

Here I am, why waste time wanting to be somewhere else?

We all spend far too much of our lives trying to get somewhere else. We dream of the next vacation, of the next promotion, of the next relationship, of the next car, of the next iPhone. We do this for an entirely sensible reason: the vast majority of our life is not what we wish it were. We struggle to be content with where we are because we are so concerned about where we are going. The problem with this way of living is that it causes us to be nearly entirely occupied with external accomplishments as the key to meaningful existence. This basic idea is the main cultural "logic," we might say, by which we make sense of our lives. According to this model, we are primed to think that in order to make where I am worthwhile it has to be leading somewhere else . . . to the next promotion, the next award, the next round of applause. And that "somewhere else" must be visible to others in ways that allow them to celebrate my being there. Only then can we claim to be "successful." As so many of our coaches, teachers, parents, politicians, and professors keep reminding us, "success" is the goal, right?! In this book I will refer to this way of living as the "success-oriented" approach.

According to the success-orientation, only if we achieve X, or do Y, or obtain Z do we think that we will *have* enough, indeed, ever *be* enough. Yet, as David Foster Wallace (2009) so aptly explains, this approach to living will inevitably leave us empty. We will never have, do, or be enough to satisfy the insatiable hunger for more, for the next thing, for what we lack.

Listen to how Wallace cashes this idea out in relation to the idea of "worship":

In the day-to-day trenches of adult life, there is actually no such thing as atheism. There is no such thing as not worshipping. Everybody worships. The only choice we get is *what* to worship. And an outstanding reason for choosing some sort of god or spiritual-type thing to worship . . . is that pretty much anything else you worship will eat you alive. If you worship money and things . . . then you will never have enough. Never feel you have enough. It's the truth. Worship your own body and beauty and sexual allure and you will always feel ugly, and when time and age start showing, you will die a million deaths before they finally plant you. (Wallace 2009, pp. 98-106)

His point here is that the object of our worship defines us. What we worship is ultimately where we find real worth. It is what constitutes what we consider "worthy." In the end, what we worship matters because it will name who we will end up becoming. Such things matter because we don't have an infinite amount of time to decide what is worth worshiping. We are finite and so our decisions are weighty.

However, how often do we take a step back, slow down, silence our phones and ask, really ask ourselves: *"what is worthy of my finitude?"*

Only when we ask that question can we begin to take seriously that life is not best understood as a task of external accomplishments— getting jobs, getting married, getting a house, getting a car, getting a reputation, getting a retirement fund, etc. Instead, and in distinction from the cultural logic of the success-oriented approach, life is better conceived as a task of "becoming a self." Another way of asking what is worthy of your finitude is: "Who are you becoming?"

These existential questions are not focused on success as the standard of meaning, but instead encourage us toward what I will term a "faithfulness-orientation" according to which joy is grounded in the lived task of self-making. The goal is not to have this or to do that in order to make our lives significant, but rather constantly to live toward what we think is worthy of our finitude, our time, our life itself. In this way, we avoid the temptation to be done with living before life is done with us. Or, as Henry David Thoreau writes, I should strive to live so that I would not "when I came to die, discover that I had not lived" (Thoreau 1993, p. 75).

I am a philosopher and so I tend to think about these issues and to ask these questions in terms of existential philosophy. In particular, the 19th Century Danish philosopher, Søren Kierkegaard, is someone to whom I frequently turn as I try to wrestle with my *own* existence, with what matters *in* existence, with why it matters that *I* exist. It is Kierkegaard who encourages us all to take seriously the task of "becoming a self," and it is Kierkegaard who I am paraphrasing in my account of faithfulness as a way of life.

Yet, I am not *only* a philosopher. I am also a fisherman, a mountain biker, an avid camper and hiker. So, when I read Kierkegaard and the other existential philosophers, I can't help but think that their frequent use of mountain metaphors, their references to rivers, their mentions of hiking, etc., are not simply coincidental but essential aspects of their reflections on lives well lived.

I readily admit that it is easy to be philosophical while sitting here by the campfire, far from the "din of towns and cities" of which William Wordsworth warns. However, philosophy is not something to be done occasionally, but instead is meant to be a way of life that facilitates intentional reflection on how to live well.

In our busy lives, we tend just to accept as "given" or "obvious" whatever value theory is operative in our broader social context. Whatever "they" say matters is what we just take for granted as mattering for us. It is as if we are all still in middle school trying to be accepted by the "cool kids." The history of philosophy is effectively a long meditation on the emptiness and futility of trying to be "cool."

Rather than worrying about what the cool kids think, Socrates suggests that we should be only concerned about what virtuous people think. In other words, we should be careful not only to think well about what is worthy of our finitude, but also about to whom we turn as we try to figure that out. In other words, almost as important as going hiking is making sure to hike with the right folks.

We are relational beings and our vulnerability is not meant to be borne alone. This is a lesson that can be learned both by reading existential philosophy and also by spending time in mountains.

In this book I will try to do a bit of both by introducing you to some philosophers that I think are worth our attention and our time as we think about these important issues. This is not meant to be an introduction to philosophy in a formal sense. Instead, it is meant to be an invitation to become a philosopher in your own life such that philosophy becomes what we do every single day as we try to live toward joy.

That said, I admit that existential philosophers are not often the best people with whom literally to go camping. Folks like Nietzsche and Kierkegaard were infamously melancholic and probably pretty miserable people to be around for long periods of time. In fact, a theologian friend of mine recently joked about this book that he couldn't imagine being "alone in a tent with Kierkegaard" and it going well. Ha! I get the joke and it is a good one.

In many ways, Kierkegaard is the last person I want to take camping with me. However, his work (and the work of other existential philosophers) is, I believe, a profound resource for living well both in the office and at the campsite. I go camping, fishing, mountain biking, hiking, offroading, etc., because these activities allow me to prioritize faithful living wherever I am. In some sense, by spending time in the mountains, by rivers, and on trails, I am able to bring the mountains and rivers back with me to the office in ways that transform the everyday into something more compelling. As Kierkegaard says, the "knight of faith" is able to find the "sublime in the pedestrian." I may fail to do that most days, but the hope remains a motivation that propels me forward. Importantly, then, "going camping with Kierkegaard" is not meant to be literal, but rather a metaphorical encouragement to be purposive about how we live, who we are becoming, and why it matters.

I just threw another log on the fire and in the process burnt my hand a bit. Finitude is marked not only by the task of meaning-making, but also by embodied vulnerability. Our bodies age, they break, they eventually die. This is part of the deal. Being human is not something to try to overcome, but instead something to try to inhabit more fully.

Living into such "fullness" is the hope of this book. I am writing it not to teach you something, but as Walt Whitman might say, to "invite my soul" toward goodness, toward beauty, and toward truth. I am writing this book because I need to think through these things, not just once and for all, but again and again. Maybe you do too? Come, let's walk together and talk along the way.

Even being here by the campfire is a divergence from the vast majority of my life up to this point. Although I love fishing—I actually got my Ph.D. to be a professor so that I could fish in the summers—I have spent far more time in pursuit of a career that would *eventually, one day, ultimately* facilitate time fishing. 80-hour work weeks have been all too normal for me ever since I was in my mid-20s. I am now 45 and have been married over 20 years. My wife, Vanessa, and I have a 13-year-old son, Atticus. Although I am an advocate of hard work and celebrate excellence as a virtue worth cultivating in our professional lives, it brings me shame to realize that most of what I have gotten for all those hours, all those years, is stress, anxiety, and time away from both my family and the mountains that I love.

When the COVID pandemic hit in 2020, something broke in me. Finitude seemed all too real. Vulnerability seemed an unmanageable burden. Far too many of us, myself included, were wrecked by the isolation, the despair, the fear, the interruption of our success-oriented lives.

I realized that the philosophy that I had taught for 20 years was not something that I was putting into practice in my own life. So, I resolved to change things. As everyone was trying to "get back to normal," I decided that maybe "normal" was not something to long for in the first place. In the midst of global chaos and unspeakable suffering (in many ways facilitated and deepened by the egoism and incompetence of our political and religious leaders), there emerged narratives of human greatness: staggering displays of charity, of empathy, of self-sacrifice, and of kindness that broke through the fear and selfishness.

For my part, I was inspired by the Italians singing to each other out of windows during quarantine, by health-care workers risking their lives in the face of uncertainty to care for the sick, and by the tragically underpaid and mistreated "essential" workers who continued to show up to their jobs so that the rest of us could safely stay home.

I was overwhelmed with the realization that since we do not have an infinite amount of time, it really matters what we do with the time that we have. "What is worthy of my finitude?" was no longer an abstract question for the philosophy classroom. It transformed into the urgent question "What will *I* do with my finitude?" and it became a matter of *daily* decision.

So I determined to make it a priority to go to the mountains. I took my son to the mountains (one of the few benefits of virtual school). I bought a mountain bike and new backpacking gear. I stopped viewing "work" as the thing that prevented me from camping, and instead decided to go camping with Kierkegaard so that I could do my work more effectively, more existentially honestly, more purposively. I decided not simply to be a philosophy *professor*, but to strive to become a *philosopher*. I realized that a success-orientation might make me money, but it would cost me my existence. This was a price I was no longer willing to pay. I don't need a Porsche, but wow this hot chocolate is good. My priorities got resituated as my identity got reshaped.

I realize that in many ways it is due to the social privilege that I inhabit that I was so easily able to buy the new gear and it is due to the flexibility of being a tenured Full Professor that I was so easily able to spend so much time on the rivers and sleeping in tents. But, awareness of this privilege just makes me even more committed to the importance of working toward a world marked by social justice that facilitates this flexibility and agency for everyone.

The brokenness that COVID made visible also illustrated the brokenness of our society and the despair that has been felt by so many for so long (especially within historically marginalized communities). Existential philosophy, for all its flaws, is right about the radical contingency of existence. "Normal" is neither obvious nor necessary. The world can and should be different.
We can change things.

I am convinced that such change starts in small ways in our daily lives. It is for that reason that I see this book as an invitation for us all to think carefully about how we are spending our lives, how we orient our projects, how we form our beliefs, and how we understand meaning.

As I try to make clear in the chapters that follow, going camping, fishing, biking, and hiking are simply my preferred ways to facilitate this sort of intentional existential reflection. These are the activities that bring me joy, that allow finitude not to be something that I desire to escape, but something that I hope to inhabit more effectively. They call to me and I try my best to respond to them.

But, and this is important, *these specifics may not be your preferred activities.* The point is not that you literally go camping (with Kierkegaard or with your family), but that you become existentially aware, that you live on purpose, that you strive toward faithfulness however you understand that to make sense in your own situation.

In metaphorical ways, and if you live near the Carolinas, maybe in literal ones as well, I hope that you will join me here by the campfire—like the large crow that is now walking toward me and the squirrels who continue to play in the trees nearby. We don't have to talk about philosophy the whole time, but maybe we can live philosophically together . . . on the trails, at the offices, and in our homes.

Come on over. I have an extra cup. I will heat up some more water for another hot chocolate. The marshmallows are on the table over there. Grab one and I will get you a stick for roasting. The air continues to be chilly, but there is warmth here by the fire. The shadows model for us how not simply to walk heavily through our lives, but to dance together on the trails.

1

What Is Worthy Of Your Finitude?

I have never thru-hiked the Appalachian Trail. I have never taken a floatplane to fish for salmon in Alaska. I have never taken my truck off-roading in Moab. I have never ridden my mountain bike at Whistler. I have never kayaked class 5+ whitewater.

I have never done any of these things. But I do spend every minute that I can in the mountains. I am an avid trout fisherman. I feel comfortable mountain biking black diamond trails in Pisgah National Forest. I do off-road in my 4x4 Tacoma (which is lifted and built out specifically for off-road capability). I have kayaked a lot of class 3 rivers (with the rare class 4 run that scares me and sends me back to the calmer waters).

The difference in what I have not done and what I do regularly is that the former are all accomplishments that one can check off as having reached the pinnacle of some particular activity. The latter, alternatively, are not things on my to-do list, but are for me important elements in a way of life devoted to experiences that facilitate joy.

Now, look, I do hope to do some fishing in Alaska, develop the abilities to feel comfortable riding at Whistler, and get my truck to some places I have never seen before (the class 5+ rapids are best left to others!). But more important than doing those things is being committed to something just as arduous and infinitely more satisfying: attempting to become a person who cultivates a life oriented toward what matters. In this way, I am seeking to live faithfully as a daily practice, rather than just dying as someone who once in a while had faith.

Lots of folks talk about faith in all sorts of ways. We often hear of the importance of "faith over fear" (usually from people trying to justify being selfish and unconcerned about others), or that "faith is taking the first step even when you can't see the whole staircase" (Martin Luther King, Jr.), or that "faith is the substance of things hoped for and the evidence of things not seen" (Hebrews 11). But sadly, faith gets all too often confused for religious belief, on the one hand, and contrasted with doubt, on the other hand. This way of approaching things misses the existential importance of understanding faithfulness as a valuable way of life for all of us regardless of our religious identity.

It is true that faith is often understood, enacted, and applied in the context of religious life, and as someone who identifies as religious (for what it is worth, I am a Pentecostal Christian), I deeply respect this particular manifestation of how faith can be enacted. Similarly, it is often the case that doubt, fear, anxiety, and worry override our ability to move forward with purpose. Finding ways to live faithfully certainly does require rethinking the hold things have on us in all sorts of ways. Nonetheless, faith is not simply, or even primarily, about religion. Similarly, faith rarely roots out our doubts, but instead it usually requires us to own up to them. Many non-religious people live faithfully day in and day out, and many religious people fail to live faithfully.

Far too often we think that we need faith in order to overcome risk, but such a view actually short-circuits itself. The real threat to faithful living is the idea that one can have certainty about things of existential importance. Faith goes hand in hand with risk, but in a way that is akin to humility being the ground of confidence. As Socrates shows, true confidence is not thinking that you are the greatest, but instead realizing that you are limited and in need of correction and encouragement from others. But, when such humility is deployed as a virtue, it allows confidence to emerge in the light of self-honesty. Living faithfully does not remove our doubts and position us as certain about ourselves, the world, and what matters. Instead, faithful living facilitates being able to act on purpose and with confidence while abandoning the idol of certainty.

As a philosopher, I think clear definitions are important. Without them we can often find ourselves missing each other's points as well as missing out on going deeper in our own thinking. So, here is my definition of faith: *risk with direction.*

Risk: No matter what we do in life, risk attends it all. Sometimes the risk is more obvious—as in the case of double black diamond mountain bike trails, class 6 rapids, and 2,190 mile hikes—but even if we sit at home in order to be maximally safe from all that would threaten us, we risk missing out on the experiences that would have given meaning to our lives in ways we could not have anticipated from the "safety" of our couches. We need to realize that such "safety" is an illusion. Risk is ubiquitous for finite beings like us. The real trick is finding ways to navigate such risk in ways that are existentially appropriate.

Risk aversion is not necessarily bad; it can serve to keep us awake and fully invested in what we are doing (despite the risks that remain). Indeed, if we did not have any risk aversion, then we would not be epistemically responsible, or true to what we do *know* (from the Greek *episteme*, or knowledge). Knowing what risks are worth taking and what risks are not worth taking is part of what Aristotle would call "practical wisdom" (*phronesis*). Developing such practical wisdom facilitates virtue because it requires that we not only

3

attend to where we are, but also requires that we pay attention to where we are hoping to go.

A quick look at the self-help books would lead you to believe that there is a one-size-fits-all sort of answer to living well. Even if that account sells a lot of books—because it traffics in the lowest common denominator sort of thinking—it is essentially and finally false. We are all different, and becoming virtuous requires us to live the life that makes the most sense for us as individuals-in-community, and therefore practical wisdom is not just a matter of learning stuff, but of cultivating deep self-awareness. Such self-awareness is always relational. We learn who we are only by attending to our social context. In this way, practical wisdom provides a sense for how to navigate well through the world. How we relate to risk is going to vary from person to person, but that we relate to risk is a part of the human condition that we all share. Faithfulness embraces risk, and it does so reflectively.

With Direction: In addition to his account of practical wisdom, Aristotle also suggests that part of what it means to live is to be capable of movement. Without wanting to get into the details about what he meant by such movement and how it should get cashed out in the context of contemporary bioethics, etc., I do think that he was on to something when it comes to the notion of movement as a matter of purpose, aim, or directionality. Aristotle's term for such directional movement is *telos*. As such, humans are intrinsically teleological beings in that we understand ourselves as purposive.

Think about how often you probably have seen college courses, community groups, or books on "finding your life's purpose." Indeed, Proverbs 29:18 says that, "where there is no vision, the people perish." Here the biblical author is hitting on the same point as Aristotle. As finite beings, our lives are measured. Whether that measurement is made in tracking significant events (graduations, birthdays, promotions, etc.), coffee spoons (as T.S. Eliot would perhaps recommend), or something more trivial like money (as most college administrators, politicians, and CEOs seem to believe), human lives are necessarily directional precisely because they are finite. If we were infinite then we would always have time to do everything and so measuring time and significance would be not only unnecessary, but also probably irrational. But, we are not immortals. And it is a good thing that we are not. As the philosopher Todd May (2017) suggests, infinity (when understood as simply a life like we experience currently but unending) would be boring and meaningless. It is because we have limited time that it matters that we measure our lives in ways that are oriented in a direction that we consider worthwhile.

Risk with direction.
That's faith.

The easy part is getting the definition. The hard part is figuring out how to implement it in one's life. Understanding faith as a concept is very different than learning to live faithfully—navigating the risk while being properly directed. Two things, in particular, have been incredibly useful in helping me figure out this living side of things (even if only partially and fallibly): (1) going camping and (2) reading Kierkegaard. Drawing inspiration from existential philosophy (and especially from Kierkegaard) while spending time in the mountains, this book is an attempt to find joy in the midst of so many temptations to despair.

It is about cultivating a life of faithfulness, rather than simply a list of successes.
It is about becoming, rather than just being.
It is about hope, rather than just accomplishments.

What is true for grilling steaks is also apt for finite human existence: there is a very fine line between being done and being ruined. Although this book probably won't be of much help when it comes to campfire cooking, hopefully it will be of some benefit when it comes to living faithfully and finding joy in the process. When all is said and done, the question we all must ask ourselves is: *what is worthy of my finitude?*

This book is an attempt to think with philosophers about this question and then seeking to apply the wisdom that they teach.

Let's get started.

The other day I bought a new mountain bike (a Kona Process 134DL for any of you who are also bikers). Understandably, I wanted to keep it looking good despite all the rocks, roots, and other obstacles that I will run it over. So, I bought some vinyl protective tape to put on the frame in order to try to prevent rock chips and scratches. Well, I got everything ready and put the first piece on the chainstay and then got ready to put another piece on the footstay. For the life of me, I simply could not get the vinyl to come off of the backing paper. I tried everything . . . for nearly 45 minutes. I had read something online that said it could be tricky to get off and so I just kept at it. Eventually every corner was bent up so badly that I had to cut them all down in order to keep trying. I was getting frustrated because not only did the piece no longer fit the area I was planning to put it on, but I just couldn't figure out how I was going to be able to do the whole bike if it was taking me 45 minutes just to get this one piece done. Well, in exasperation I called for my wife, Vanessa, and in near Sartrean despair I handed it to her and asked for help. She looked at it for no more than 15 seconds and then said, "Are you sure that this is a new piece and not simply the paper left over from a piece you have already used?" Although I immediately responded with incredulous disdain for her assumption that I could be that dumb, it didn't take me long to realize that she was right. Oooof.

There are a bunch of lessons that could be learned here, and what stands out to me are two things that can help us as we think together about living faithfully:

1. Persistence is not a virtue if it is misguided.
2. Relational existence requires humility.

Lesson 1: On Misguided Persistence

We often hear that persistence is a virtue. But like most things in human existence, it depends. It depends on what we are persisting toward. Think back to Aristotle's notion of directional movement. Persistence means staying true to something that is not easily attained. And yet, we sometimes forget there are lots of things that are both difficult and definitely not worth attaining! There are easy examples, of course, such as persisting toward being the best bully on the playground, or toward being the best thief. Harder examples are things like persisting on the path toward medical school when you continue to struggle with science courses. Should you just grit your teeth, dig in, and work harder for what you want? Maybe you need to admit that there is a disconnection between what you want and what your abilities/talents/skills make possible. Alternatively, consider the businessperson who is currently a mid-manager, but in line for a major promotion. Let's assume that this person has always dreamed of being a Vice-President of a large company. She is now within striking distance of that goal, but the long hours have come at a significant cost to other things in her life. Should she persist toward the position even if it comes at costs that, upon reflection, she probably might not be willing to pay?

These are hard cases because they do not admit of clear answers regarding what the right thing to do actually is (remember that the idol of certainty is a cruel master). Though there might be resources available in philosophy to help remove some concerns and provide some general framework for virtue, there is no algorithm for living well. *Responsibility is messy because embodiment is.* Moreover, the difficulty of responsible existence is due to our being free. If we did not have agency to choose otherwise, then there would be no problems trying to figure out what we should do. If you think that this sounds like a good alternative world, be careful what you wish for. Without agency, our finitude would be meaningless. It is only because our embodied finitude is characterized by freedom that choosing this instead of that matters. Ultimately, the choice is indeed yours (as the rap group Black Sheep might say). It is in choosing wisely that we actively write the narrative of our lives that will be read by others.

Freedom = Risk
Risk = Faith
Freedom = Faith

Now, we could claim that even if it is good that we have agency, it would be better if we had clearer guidance on how to make the best choices. Remember that scene at the end of *Indiana Jones and the Last Crusade*? You know the one—where the characters are faced with the choice of which cup was used by Christ at the Last Supper. There are lots of options (freedom is only morally significant if there are alternatives that could be actualized), and there is the old knight who knows which cup is the right one. The old knight does not tell them which to choose, though. If he did, then there would still be freedom, but no risk. And remember, if there is no risk, then there is no faith. Freedom matters because we can, as the old knight says, "choose poorly."

Jean-Paul Sartre nicely addresses the riskiness of freedom when he claims that we are "condemned to be free." In this (in)famous phrase, he acknowledges the fact that it seems like things would be much better if we were not so free, or at least wiser in the face of our freedom (i.e., had a knight to guide us). Sartre offers an interesting example of the radicality of choice that might be helpful for our consideration of the complexities that attend the importance of persisting only toward that which is worthwhile. He tells a story about one of his students who lived with his mother because of estrangement from his father. His older brother had been killed in the war, and so he was now singularly responsible for caring for his mom. Sartre then explains the situation as follows:

> The boy was faced with the choice of leaving for England and joining the Free French Forces—that is, leaving his mother behind—or remaining with his mother and helping her to carry on. He was fully aware that the woman lived only for him and

that his going-off—and perhaps his death—would plunge her into despair. He was also aware that every act that he did for his mother's sake was a sure thing, in the sense that it was helping her to carry on, whereas every effort he made toward going off and fighting was an uncertain move which might run aground and prove completely useless . . . . As a result, he was faced with two very different kinds of action: one, concrete, immediate, but concerning only one individual; the other concerned an incomparably vaster group, a national collectivity, but for that very reason was dubious, and might be interrupted on route. And, at the same time, he was wavering between two kinds of ethics. On the one hand, an ethics of sympathy, of personal devotion; on the other, a broader ethics, but one whose efficacy was more dubious. He had to choose between the two. (Sartre 1985, pp. 24-25)

Here we see Sartre admitting that both options have benefits, such that each could be characterized as the morally preferable option, and yet both come at costs that forestall any easy conscience about choosing one instead of the other. Sartre then asks the question that we are now asking about persistence: "Who could help him choose?" (Sartre 1985, p. 25). Here he is looking for some old knight who might have the moral wisdom that eliminates the risk attendant to moral freedom. After considering some options (namely, Christian doctrine and ethical theories), he concludes that none are up to the task because they all just raise further questions of judgment. If he is to love his neighbor, say, then *who* is his neighbor—his mother or his countrypersons? If he appeals to Kantian ethics, alternatively, then *which* other is the one that he is treating as an end rather than as a means—again, his mother or his countrypersons?

Perhaps we follow a more Aristotelian approach and seek out a moral exemplar who could help us make better decisions? Well, doing so already implicates us in having some criterion of judgment. Sartre rightly recognizes that "choosing your advisor is involving yourself" (Sartre 1985, p. 27). His claim is that there is no value-neutral way to assess values. We are always already enmeshed. So, as much as we might wish that we could find the old knight to guide us, part of what makes the old knight relevant to our specific case is the judgment that he has the right sort of knowledge, or wisdom. In other words, maybe the knight is really just a jester in stolen armor? Distinguishing between the knight and the jester is not something we can ask the knight/jester to do for us.

The point is that even when it seems that moral guidance is available, we are faced with the complicated reality of agency and uncertainty, which again means that risk remains regardless of the direction we choose to pursue.

Ultimately, Sartre concludes that, "the only thing left is for us to trust our instincts" (Sartre 1985, p. 26). Though folks like William James and Ralph Waldo Emerson might applaud this affective model, I think it is also just as fraught as the options that Sartre dismisses.

Again, some choices are more easily made than others. Choosing between jumping off the roof of a multi-story building or going to the ice cream shop is not usually a decision that requires much reflective judgment. Indeed, in such "easy cases" we might even suggest that there is no instance of authentic decision in the first place. Jacques Derrida suggests something along this line when he claims that decision is only possible when faced with what he terms "the undecidable." For Derrida, the undecidable is like the situation of the student considering whether to go to war or stay and care for his mother. Both options are plausibly good, and both are plausibly bad. Decision is now required because there is an objectively undecidable challenge. Action is mandated by the fact that the right way forward is not clear. Ethical ambiguity, as Simone de Beauvoir would term it, is not a contingent part of moral life, but an essential quality of relational existence for finite, embodied, vulnerable beings like us.

One of my former professors and mentors, David Kangas, said the following during a course I took with him on existentialist ethics. Notice that he uses the concept of incommensurability to indicate that there is not always a common scale of measurement by which competing values can be compared:

> The difficulty of moral choice is not only the uncertainty of consequences of our actions, but also the reality of the incommensurability of two opposing choices. There is nothing that triumphs over this ambiguity. No moral system allows us to triumph over the paradox of ethical anxiety.

I have that quote from Kangas written on the back cover of my copy of Sartre's *Existentialism and Human Emotions*. I often return to it when I am wrestling with moral questions in my own life. I always read it to my students when I teach Sartre. I guess that this makes Kangas something of a wise old knight to whom I turn, but notice that his words are not that this or that would be "choosing wisely" or "choosing poorly." His wisdom is that of Socrates, he knows that he doesn't have it all figured out and so facilitates an awareness of the weight of risky decision. This is the sort of moral exemplar I find compelling. He is not there to tell me/us what to do, but to remind me/us of the solidarity that attends human vulnerability.

We are in this together precisely because of the variety of futures into which we could collectively live. If our lives were defined by necessity, then there would be no need for relational solidarity as a mode of encouragement. There would similarly be no need for decision because there would be no agency. Because we are free, our lives are risky. Because our lives are risky, our futures are contingent. Because our futures are contingent, things might go wrong or right depending on what world we choose to make real. There is no obvious future toward which we should strive, but rather a variety of futures that would all be desirable, as well as others that would not. Only because there is no objective place from which to make such decision is real decision possible. Otherwise, as Derrida illuminates, it wouldn't be ethical decision, it would just be math.

How can we apply these general moral lessons to persistence? Well, [*always* choosing to persist can quickly lead to bad outcomes] In such cases, it is hard to see how it is virtuous if the result is frustration, suffering, harm, and possibly even death. Persisting toward the promotion at the cost of one's family, persisting toward the end of the trail at the cost of starvation, persisting toward the degree and career at the cost of happiness, etc.—these are not examples of virtuous endurance. [People who choose to persist in such cases are not to be admired, but rather pitied] They should be pitied because they didn't admit of the reality of decision. They were deceived into thinking that persistence is always a good.

This is a tempting thought, but life isn't that simple. Persistence matters only if that toward which one persists is worth the risk of seeking it.

Walt Whitman writes a poem in which he lists things that bring joy. Therein he proclaims, in the tone of existential longing:

> O to struggle against great odds, to meet enemies undaunted!
> To be entirely alone with them, to find how much one can stand!
> To look strife, torture, prison, popular odium, face to face!
> To mount the scaffold, to advance to the muzzles of guns with perfect nonchalance!
> To be indeed a God![2]

As much as I love this selection from Whitman (and believe me, I love it!—maybe I watched *Dead Poets Society* too many times, sigh), we must remember that the last line is the important one. "To be indeed a God" amounts to the Nietzschean idea that the death of

---

2   Walt Whitman, "Song of Joys," from *Leaves of Grass*. Available at https://whitmanarchive.org/published/LG/1881/poems/90. Accessed May 26, 2023.

God is the birth of our responsibility. This is not a claim about the truth of atheism, but about the truth of finding ourselves in spaces that demand decision despite a lack of clarity. Whitman's idea, as is the case for Nietzsche, is that gods are essentially creative. Gods not only create objects, but values. In this sense, gods decide what will have meaning and what will not. We must be "a God" in order to take up the task of world creation that attends the decision required in the face of ethical anxiety.

Anyone who has recently taken a college admissions tour is, no doubt, familiar with the claim that colleges claim to offer "real world experiences." Who could be opposed to that? Isn't this the sort of experiential education that John Dewey recommends over the traditionalist model of just being expected to memorize facts? Well, the problem is not with such experiences, but that such experiences are described as reflecting the "real world." Whitman, Nietzsche, Sartre, Derrida, Beauvoir, and Kangas would all respond in chorus that *there is no real world, there is only the world that we have chosen to make real.*

When we realize this, that we are world-creators, meaning-makers, "Gods," then we will balk at the ease with which college administrators, public relations officers, and usually the parents of prospective students, all assume that the world is such that decision is easy because there is a way that things are, and a teachable cultural logic of success that governs those things. We would do well to remember that even physics eventually runs up against the uncertainty principle, that math faces the incompleteness theorems, and that history is a story told from particular perspectives all with interests that complicate any narrative of objectivity.

Again, we confront the core question: What will you do with your finitude? This question can be restated as: What world will you decide to make real? This way of putting things is unlikely to resonate as easily in the ears of the privileged, who deceive themselves into believing that their way of envisioning the world is simply the way that things are, but it speaks to the truth of philosophical awareness.

Lesson 2: Humility is Hard Work

Aristotle once said that it is hard work to be excellent. Well, he should have added that humility is hard work as well (maybe this is why Kendrick Lamar devoted a whole song to stressing its importance). Pointing out how hard humility is might seem like an odd claim in a time when so many people struggle with self-confidence. Given the significant realities of anxiety, depression, social shaming, and bullying, it might appear that finding the strength to be self-confident is the harder task. However, I tend to see it the other way around. We struggle with self-confidence precisely because we have allowed arrogance to become culturally normative. In other words, folks who might otherwise be appropriately humble tend to feel like they are worthless because they don't walk around with their chests puffed out like so many others do. Sadly, we tend to view those arrogant others in ways that make it difficult to critique their vice. In particular, we change the domain in which we assess their behavior. Rather than considering it in a moral register, we locate it internal to a broadly economic logic that reads everything through a lens of "success." That lens is so ubiquitous that it can sometimes be hard to see it. But, here are some indicators of how it shows up:

- They are not arrogant, our society might say, they are just really good at what they do.
- They are not cocky, society continues, they are just willing to do what it takes to get ahead in a competitive environment.
- You are not humble in virtuous ways, society then adds, you are just jealous of their success.

So, instead of recommending humility, we tell the people displaying it to stop being "haters." Accordingly, rather than embracing virtue, we give in to the worst of our own self-doubts.

Aaron James diagnoses our situation exceptionally well when he says that we live in an "asshole culture" underwritten by "asshole capitalism." Let's spend just a few minutes getting clear on his account in order then to return to the idea of humility as moral and epistemic virtue that stands as something of a potential cultural corrective to the dangerous road on which we now find ourselves.

In his striking book, *Assholes*, James does what all good philosophers do (and what we did at the beginning of this book)—he gives definitions for the central terms he will be using. When it comes to the term 'asshole', it might seem that we all know what we are talking about when we use the word. And, since we use it so often for so many people, it stands to reason that we are very clear about its meaning. As David Foster Wallace constantly reminds us, however, what seems the most obvious is usually the most fraught and in need of careful thinking. What seems obvious strikes us as such simply because it's so common, or so pervasive. Accordingly, we either become oblivious to it, or have thousands of different takes on it, either scenario leads either to vagueness or confusion.

When it comes to the idea of "assholes," our over-usage of the term has led to a near ubiquitous application that has stretched its meaning in ways that undermine its semantic traction. That is, when a word means nearly anything, it doesn't mean much at all. To correct things, James gives a very specific definition. An asshole, he says, is someone who:

1. allows himself to enjoy special advantages and does so systematically;
2. does this out of an entrenched sense of entitlement; and
3. is immunized by his sense of entitlement against the complaints of other people. (James 2012, p. 5)

Notice that this three-part definition rules out a variety of things in the attempt to be quite philosophically precise. It helps us to distinguish between those moments in your life when you "act like an asshole" as opposed to people who "are assholes." This difference is crucial and indicated in James's stress on the idea of systematic and entrenched sense of entitlement. The fact is that assholes are not people who occasionally give in to the vice of arrogance or inappropriate self-interest (this is good news, since we all would be guilty of such occasional egoism!), but instead assholes are those who always do so. Their very character has become compromised, we might say. They are immunized against complaints and criticisms from others precisely because they no longer consider others to be of equal moral standing. "What on earth could *you* possibly say to *me*?", "Don't you know who *I* am?", the asshole declares atop his high horse.

Such a sweeping diminution of others is not something about which the asshole feels guilty. Instead, the asshole does not recognize the others as equals such that guilt would be an appropriate moral emotion. The asshole, thus, sees all others as tools to be used for personal benefit. These others are, as Simone Weil (2005) would say, reduced to "things." And, since the asshole sees the world through an economic lens, these others/things are worthwhile only insofar as they serve the purpose of increased profits (whether those profits be understood in terms of money, power, privilege, or status). As a negative characterization, we might say that an asshole refuses any existential draw of what Martin Buber (1970) calls the "I-Thou" relationship. Assholes are always, instead, in "I-It" relationships within a perspective where their own moral sense is taken as sacrosanct without qualification. Their own judgment is felt to be infallible. Their own interests are taken to be absolute and beyond challenge.

Now, one might quickly respond that there have always been assholes and so why should we spend so much time thinking about these social pariahs. Well, remember that all of this discussion emerged in the attempt to defend the claim that humility is hard work in a society where assholes have become socially normative. At an existential level, it is not this or that asshole that presents the ultimate problem (even when a specific and glaringly obvious asshole has enormous power). Rather, the real issue is the social logic by which assholes are re-narrated as successful models of human flourishing. This social logic is what James means by "asshole capitalism."

It is the idea that being an asshole is now just assumed to be what it takes to get ahead in society, and so assholery is no longer a moral failure, but simply a reflection of what we need to cultivate if we are to achieve our social/material/cultural goals.

Notice how seductive and dangerous this situation is. The systematic and entrenched sense of entitlement is not a problematic characteristic of some individuals we can simply choose to avoid so far as possible. Instead, it is the very goal of social accomplishment presented as worthy of our existential striving. Similarly, becoming immune from criticism is not now a regrettable characteristic of some people we hope not to have as bosses, say, but instead is woven into the very fabric of social life. Critique is narrated as dissention, disloyalty, and dishonor.

Socrates was right when he said that [offering critique to a friend is how you care about the soul of another.]Friendship (whether as an interpersonal reality or a social framework) is a matter of moral equality that facilitates moral critique.[Genuine humility grounds appropriate self-confidence because humble people love truth more than being right.]That is hard work indeed. Yet, truth, goodness, and beauty are always connected to difficult work that is worth undertaking—they are directions worthy of the risk involved.

If our social narrative is one that facilitates assholes because success is no longer about being someone of upright character whose confidence is grounded in both humility and also a recognition of the moral dignity of all others, then our society is on the road to ruin. Look, I fully expect that some of you will hear this as a call for some sort of traditionalist ethics and instantly confuse my voice with that of your grandmother asking you where you have been and why you are coming in so late. I get it. It can be tough to think about a moral life in a context when so many defending "family values" stand against the rights of their neighbors, and those who describe themselves as "values voters" tend to be those who care only about the value of reinforcing their own social status at the cost of those who are historically marginalized. In such a confusing rhetorical space, it can seem like the only way to stand for moral life is to stop calling for moral living.

However, I don't think that we need to throw the baby out with the bathwater quite so quickly. Doing so would be based on what philosophers term a "non-sequitur." That is, it would be assuming that one thing entails, or logically requires, something else when it simply doesn't. In this case, we can realize that we need a moral critique of our social norms without necessarily embracing the prominent form in which such social moralism tends to be presented quite loudly in popular culture.

Nuance is difficult when everyone defines themselves using filters on Instagram and discovers their voice by shouting about things on Twitter (or X, or whatever Elon Musk decides to name it next month). Critique is difficult when half the population (this cuts in both directions, by the way) is worried about being canceled. Moral life is difficult when "character-building" is so often a euphemism for toxic masculinity grounded in theological complementarianism. And yet, Instagram might be an important social tool, lots of behavior and beliefs deserve to be canceled, and theology could even be a resource for overcoming patriarchy in various ways. Easy dichotomies are at odds with faithfulness as a way of life.

So, how might we begin to navigate through such troubled waters that just seem to get rougher in the midst of the "din of towns and cities," as Wordsworth would say?

We have probably all heard some version of the idea that you need the world to quiet down so that you can hear yourself think. Well, when I need to think, I go camping. There in the mountains I find an existential solace so very absent in a world controlled by assholes.

Although, personally, I use the phrase "camping in the mountains" in a literal sense, you should feel free to hear it metaphorically. That is, taken literally it is simply my preferred way of allowing question marks to show up in a life all too easily defined by periods (and even a bunch of exclamation points). Rather than simply giving in to the asshole culture of "that's just the way it is" (with apologies to Bruce Hornsby and 2Pac), I long for moments where I can ask, "How do I wish it were?" Instead of the constant nagging sense that "the real world" is grinding me under its gears, I need moments when I can ask: "What world do I think should be made real?" "Who am I becoming?" "What will I choose in the face of ethical ambiguity?"

The COVID pandemic made us all long for normal, yet what I am proposing here is that we need to interrogate what gets to count as "normal." Maybe normality for you is good and brings you joy. But in many cases it can rob us of our joy by preventing us from realizing the agency that we have in deciding how to spend our time and how to direct our effort.

And so we return to the all-important question: *What is worthy of your finitude?*

If you are reading this book, then you, like me, are not quite done with your finitude, and so the question continues to press on us all. This book is personal, in that I draw on my own experiences, but it is meant not really to be stories about my own life, but an invitation to become more invested in narrating or creating the story of *your* own life.

Whatever your career, whatever your choices, whatever your past or your plans for the future, your life will be defined by relationships, risks, hopes, fears, loss, and joy. Philosophy is essentially the attempt to take those things seriously in order to navigate them more effectively. Philosophy is then not at all irrelevant to our lives, but instead is itself, as Pierre Hadot (1995) suggests, *a way of life.*

As I see it, living philosophically is a matter of living faithfully. And

19

as most philosophers realize, we always have more thinking to do, and therefore more living to do. I sincerely believe that philosophy can and should help us to live well . . . whether in the mountains, at the beach, in the office, at home . . . whether in our role as citizen, parent, friend, student, or whatever. Regardless of our situation, the existential task is the same.

Let's review the two lessons we have learned together:

- Persistence is important when rightly directed.
- Humility is hard work.

These lessons are keys to interrupting the social stream of consciousness that so often overrides our ability to be conscious, responsible, faithful, and awake. The bands Rage Against the Machine and Lamb of God both have songs that remind us to "wake up." This is not a call to "wokeness," but a call to awareness, to reflective existence, to paying attention, to asking questions, and to finding joy.

Going to the mountains is what wakes me up.

What about you?
What wakes you up?

Maybe it is sitting on the beach (can I get an "amen" from my wife?!?). Maybe it is spending time with friends in good conversation. Maybe it is playing board games. Maybe it is reading a book. Maybe it is going surfing (keep rocking, Aaron James!). Maybe it is learning a new skill. The point is that it doesn't really matter much what it is, and it doesn't matter if I don't find your "mountain" to be one that I think is worth climbing. The point is that we have to find ways to shift our attention from the culturally defined asshole notion of "success" to the existentially weighty sense of "faithfulness."

Risk with direction.
Persistence rightly oriented.

Confidence appropriately grounded.
Finitude intentionally lived.
Questions embraced so that periods might be placed on purpose.

When we spend time in the mountains, we are constantly reminded that persistence and humility are constantly required. We have to persist on the hike, even when exhausted, to get to the overlook. We have to remain humble enough to admit that sometimes we need to turn around if the weather gets bad or the rocks get too slippery. We have to persist climbing mile after mile on our bike to get to the trailhead so that we can drop in on the downhill route. We have to remain humble enough to realize that some downhill trails are beyond our ability. We have to persist through the cold and windy night in the tent in order to get to see the sunrise from on top of the bald. We have to maintain enough humility to know when the cold and wind have become too dangerous to make the sunrise worth it.

Persistence and humility go hand in hand as part of a life lived faithfully. Don't be lulled to sleep with the alure of worldly success. When we see faithfulness as a way of life we are never done with the risk, but we can make joy our companion on the trail.

Wake up. Let's go to the mountains.

2

ALONE IN THE MOUNTAINS

Mountain metaphors are frequently used in philosophy to highlight the way that human existence is not a static sort of thing. For example, Friedrich Nietzsche talks about the importance of philosophers becoming mountain-climbers who have long legs, strong lungs, and the fortitude to live alone amidst ice and snow. His point is not quite so "cold" as it might initially seem. For Nietzsche, mountains are both literal obstacles to be overcome by human will (and he made a habit of hiking in order to foreground the activity of human will as a daily reality), and also metaphors for escaping the crowd—and the related mass of opinion that reduces us to competitive crabs pulling each other back down into the social bucket.

Nietzsche is definitely not someone to whom we should turn in the attempt to cultivate empathy, but I do think he is extremely helpful when it comes to the importance of solidarity regarding the human condition. Simply put, he appreciates that climbing mountains reveals the perhaps paradoxical reality of our simultaneous vulnerability and relational potentiality. For Nietzsche and most other philosophers who reflect on the human situation, these two aspects are different sides of the same coin. There is no potential for greatness without the risk of disaster. There is no vulnerability if everything is already perfected.

In his book, *A Fragile Life*, Todd May (2017) nicely explains that life is about trajectory. We are always moving in some direction, and rarely is that direction simply straight ahead. Usually, it is up a steep climb toward an overlook that lets us breathe deep and reflect on how far we have come, or it is a downhill slide toward what seems like a valley from which we will never escape. May's point is important because where we currently are on our particular existential trajectory (whether reaching toward the summit or crying out from the bog), we narrate the rest of our life in relation to that present moment. Where we are, *right here and right now* (yes, I admit I am singing that song by Jesus Jones now), is the only place from which to survey where we have been and where we are going. This can be an intimidating realization because it quickly invites the humility we discussed in the previous chapter. No one sits on mountaintops forever—all climbs are followed with descents (and this highlights our inevitable vulnerability). Additionally, all valleys are defined with respect to some other mountain that could be climbed (and this is our relational potentiality).

Although not usually known for his existential awareness, Rene Descartes (1998) interestingly hits on this basic idea of a necessary connection between vulnerability and potential in his "trademark" argument for God in the *Meditations*. There, he offers an argument by analogy: Just like you can't think of a mountain without a valley (and vice-versa), you can't think of God without thinking about necessary existence. Although I find this a slightly more compelling version of the ontological argument for the existence of a classical theistic God than offered by St. Anselm, I am not interested in the theological import of his example here. What stands out as relevant is that we are unable to think of mountains without valleys. In other words, there is an ontological constraint on our conceptual capacity. We can't just think anything we want. There are rational and logical limits. That very limitation is, itself, an invitation to realize our finite vulnerability.

For Descartes, infinitude represented a kind of perfection that would be free from all doubt and desire. Yet, for finite beings, our very doubts about our perfection and any desire we have to overcome such doubts via the path of inquiry and adopting a philosophical way of life highlight our vulnerability. We are the sorts of beings who think according to rules and live according to risks. We can fall off mountains, or drown in the rivers running through the valleys, and in the meantime we can be misguided in our beliefs, confused in our commitments, and overwrought in our actions.

No mountains without valleys. No valleys without mountains. This is not a claim about the need for suffering to make joy possible—I reject such theodicies as actually contributing to the amount of evil in the world—but instead a claim about the necessary connection that wherever our current position is relative to the existential trajectory of our narrated lives, we are not guaranteed that the trajectory will continue unabated. Mountains don't rise forever. Valleys eventually turn back into mountains (however slight the grade). Movement is what matters, and along with it an awareness that standing still might be an option for a classical theistic God (as illustrated by the trademark argument), but not for embodied finite beings like us.

It matters that we can be broken. Facing this reality makes it possible to celebrate those who keep walking despite the pain, who keep climbing no matter how slowly, and who encourage others along the way.

However good Nietzsche was at hiking up steep mountains in the Alps, he was not good at encouragement. As an ethical egoist, he was better at self-praise than supporting others. One of the great ironies of spending time in the mountains is that in the effort to escape the "they," the "crowd," the "public," and the "herd," we can also forget the Aristotelian warning that only beasts or gods live outside the city.

Of course, Aristotle is not praising the distinctive virtues of urban or suburban living, or the value of good civil planning for playgrounds, co-working spaces, coffee shops, and farmers markets. He is, instead, making a point about the inherently social nature of human beings. To be is to be relational. We are not meant to live alone (despite all the Discovery channel shows about Alaskan bushpeople and with all due respect to Les "Survivorman" Stroud, who is a badass, by the way). But it is important to distinguish between being alone in an *empirical* sense and being alone in an *ethical* sense.

Empirical aloneness is what camping in the mountains makes possible. Even when I go backpacking with others, I am/we are still empirically alone in the sense of being separated from the normal pacing of social existence. It is in this empirical sense that we "get away from it all."

Ethical aloneness is what characterizes the life of the asshole. The asshole lives his life as an active resistance to and rejection of what Martin Heidegger (2010) terms "being-with." Being with others is, for Heidegger, constitutive of who we are. He means this simply in a descriptive way, pointing out that our concepts, our language use, our very affirmations of meaning are all inherently social. That is, they are navigated in relationship with others, such that we never start from zero when it comes to our understanding of ourselves and the world. We receive the world as already formed, meaningful, and intelligible in particular ways that then are handed over to us as described in concrete languages, cultivated in shared practices, and then fixed in social histories. Being-with is a background assumption that makes possible being-me in specific ways as I attempt to stand out against the inherited social context. Although being-with is, for Heidegger, not a moral conception, it quickly becomes moral at the hands of many who read Heidegger—like Simone de Beauvoir and Emmanuel Levinas.

For Beauvoir (1976), being with others is a matter of becoming aware of the inescapability of ethical decision. She explains this idea

25

in her striking book, *The Ethics of Ambiguity*. Her basic idea is that human existence is radically singular; no one can make our decisions for us. Nobody can override our agency when it comes to the question of what is worthy of our finitude. But plenty of social realities can make it seem like our personal agency is quite limited in practical ways. And this is why we need a strong commitment to social justice as accompanying a commitment to faithfulness as a lived task.

However, despite such singularity, our decisions are always occasioned by and implicated in our relationships with others. What ought I to do? This is not a question that is asked in isolation, even if we are empirically alone. Our ethical sociality extends all the way down. Philosopher Judith Butler (2005) nicely speaks to this idea when she notes that the idea of selfhood, as such, amounts to our giving an account of ourselves in the face of others who implicitly demand us to provide reasons for how we navigate the world. Rationality itself is a social phenomenon for both Butler and Beauvoir. We can also compare Hannah Arendt's (1968) account of how rationality operates in a social context and Stephen Minister's (2012) idea of moral reason giving as a requirement for well-functioning societies. My point here is simply that lots of good philosophers have realized that being a self requires a deep connection with others.

Pushing beyond Beauvoir's idea of ethical ambiguity that can arise due to social relationships, Emmanuel Levinas (1969) goes as far as to say that our very subjectivity is first and foremost defined as not simply being-with, but as *being-responsible-for*. His idea is that being-with can all too quickly become an algorithmic conception of human existence that is better suited for humans-as-employees than it is for humans-as-affective-units-of-dignity. Levinas suggests that ethics goes deeper than ontology. To be is already to be responsible. He uses the idea of the "face of the other" as a phrase/image/idea that conveys the ways that we are not originally alone in our freedom and then only subsequently responsible in our social lives. Instead, freedom is, for Levinas, always a name for the fact that we have to adjudicate among competing claims on our embodied actions and decide about how to be responsible. We can't do everything for everyone. And yet we must often choose the best way to help others get on an uphill trajectory rather than getting stuck in the valley. Maybe Kate Bush's desire to keep "running up that hill," was just a good Levinasian awareness?

Ethical aloneness is a matter of refusing to see others as moral equals. Relational sociality as a defining quality of human existence is a way to avoid such egoism. Empirical aloneness is a matter of realizing that the inertia of social normativity, the cluster of habits that the crowd tends to force upon us as obvious, often overruns careful thinking and faithful living. Escaping society as a temporary possibility, in order to make way for a fuller array of human action, is a remedy.

Here's a beautiful irony, or a great paradox. Those who are the very best at empirical aloneness are often also the best at relational sociality. A good philosopher friend of mine, James Bednar, is a serious thru-hiker. I am not. I enjoy extended hiking trips, but I prefer truck camping to backpacking for a variety of reasons. And, yes, I know that for many, this may cause you to, like Liam did to Noel in the band Oasis, "turn away in anger." James always hikes with his dog, Ken Jackson. Even though James is empirically alone while on trail, in the sense that he is there on purpose as an escape from social pressures and expectations, he is never ethically alone. With Ken Jackson just a few feet ahead of him, James remains in relationship with others in his relational community back home as the context for the joy that comes from such isolation. Even when I go backpacking with James our togetherness does not erase the benefits of empirical aloneness that we experience away from society. Being on the trails together, though, does highlight the ethical relations that continue to frame our selfhood and illustrate why ethical aloneness is a failure of faithfulness, not its result.

Writing about what he terms "one of my favorite spots," Kierkegaard describes standing near the sea at one of the highest points in the area of his hikes, the region of Gilbjerget, in Denmark. His description is striking in the way that it hits on so many of the themes we have discussed up to this point. Let's just listen to his experience as he recounts it:

> Often, as I stood here of a quiet evening, the sea intoning its song with deep but calm solemnity, my eye catching not a single sail on the vast surface, and only the sea framed the sky and the sky the sea and when, too, the busy hum of life grew silent and the birds sang their vespers, then the few dear departed ones rose from the grave before me, or rather it seemed as though they were not dead. I felt so much at ease in their midst, I rested in their embrace, and I felt as though I were outside my body and floated about with them in a higher ether – until the seagull's harsh screech reminded me that I stood alone and it all vanished before my eyes, and with heavy heart I turned back to mingle with the world's throng – yet without forgetting such blessed moments. (35 I A 68; as cited in Kierkegaard 1996, p. 26).

Notice that Kierkegaard temporarily loses society and finds himself—not as ethically alone, but in a deeper and more profound relationship to others. It is both the birds singing their "vespers" that causes the "busy hum of life" to become silent, and it is also the birds harshly screeching that "reminded" him that his empirical aloneness is only ever temporary. The idea here seems to be that there is nothing magical or mystical about the specific experiential occasion for empirical aloneness. What matters is that we wake up to the contingency of how the world has been handed over to us. The birds faithfully chirp that things could be otherwise. But we must always remember that critique accompanies affirmation. The birds also reinforce how difficult it can be to hear their chirping over the blaring sounds of success. It is with a "heavy heart" that Kierkegaard "turns back" to the norms that shape his daily life. Interestingly, his walk back toward the lights and sounds of the city, and away from the lights and sounds of the seaside, is a transformed one. Being empirically alone changes things in such a way that the temptation to ethical aloneness cultivated by society is forestalled, at least for a while. He does not forget where he has walked . . . even though he now admits that it is time to turn around.

I have never enjoyed out-and-back hikes as much as I enjoy loops. I wonder if part of why I like loop hikes more is what Kierkegaard is getting at here. Hiking a loop (whether one that lasts for many miles or for just a few) allows us never to have to think much about turning around. We just keep moving forward and then eventually arrive back at the trailhead. Out-and-back hikes require us actively to retrace our steps, but now by moving in the opposite direction. That turning around is, at least for me, the hard part.

On the way up to the lookout, or out to the campsite, or down to the waterfall, or wherever the particular hike takes me, I walk with a sense of anticipation. My steps are called forward and defined by the unknown. On the way back, having turned around, I walk with a sense of accomplishment. The real adventure is mostly over. My steps are then defined by the familiar. I think that the distinction between the out and the back, as it were, is a difference between seeing our lives as a matter of becoming (faithfulness) and a matter of being (success). Even though I am writing this book as an attempt to contend for the importance of faithfulness in a world defined by success, I am not opposed to the importance of marking our goals, tracking our progress, and celebrating our victories. When it comes to hiking, *all becoming* just means you are lost! Alternatively, though, *all being* means you aren't really hiking, but just going through your daily motions with better scenery.

A caveat here is probably worthwhile. Some of my favorite hikes are ones I have done many, many times, and my favorite fishing spots are ones that I have frequented often—to the point of knowing where all the rocks are under the water and where the fish are likely to be holding their own against the current. My point about becoming and being is not meant to say that we always have to do new stuff. Indeed, an obsession with novelty is often the idolatry of contemporary capitalism. All I am trying to get at is the way that when we are setting out in anticipation, our footfalls are different than they are when we are merely turning around in exhaustion. Eschatological hope is different than economic accomplishment. When we cultivate faithfulness as a way of life, though, even the familiar is transformed—as Kierkegaard explicitly notes. Faithful living is essentially a matter of openness. Receptiveness to that openness requires not only that we are aware of the possibility of difference, but also responsive to the demands that it places on our continued becoming.

There is a particular spot on the Hiwassee River in Tennessee that my dad and I have fished more times than we can count and never had done much good, but we always returned to it because, as we would say every time, "it looks like such a fishy spot." Well, on one such return trip the water levels were different than we were expecting. The water was high and so the holes were deeper than normal. This small shift in water levels changes a bunch of other things. It means that the difference in the river's current on the surface and at the bottom will be more pronounced. It means that there are all sorts of things that have gotten washed into the river that might normally have remained on the shore just out of reach of the water. It means that the fish are less likely to be spooked by the movement of fisherman like us. It means that usually the water temperatures will be slightly lower or higher than normal, depending on the cause of the water level rise—whether from rain or from water being released from a dam. Anyway, the point is that nuance matters. That day, all sorts of things are different and just acknowledging this but then proceeding to fish that spot the way that we always did would not likely lead to a change in outcomes. With the change in water, we changed our method of fishing. To our complete surprise, we caught fish after fish and it seemed like they were just all there waiting for us to cast the line.

That was a day that my dad and I both remember extremely well and when we so regularly have to "mingle with the world's throng," as Kierkegaard says, we do so without ever forgetting such "blessed moments." We have fished that spot probably 50 more times since that eventful day and even though the water levels have been higher some days and everything seemed to be set for us to clean up again, we never have. Even though that spot only produced that one time, it remains one of my favorite places to fish and I return to it whenever I can.

These days I have to go to that spot on the Hiwassee River by myself, because my dad can't make it down the steep slope anymore due to his increased age—vulnerability and relational potentiality are not always revealed in equal measure. But, even by myself, I am never really alone. I go there in anticipation every time and my dad's company is constant even when he is miles away. It's such a fishy spot . . .

Novelty is not the point.
Openness is.

We must be willing to be surprised, but this means that we also must be open to receiving things differently than expected. One problem with success is that it is measured by expectations being met. The promise of faithfulness is that it unfazed by the adaptation required by anticipation.

I mentioned that my dad no longer can fish that particular spot with me. Even admitting this in writing as I am doing now is hard for me because it threatens to allow vulnerability to become all consuming. The blessed moments risk becoming nothing more than memories, rather than spurs to transformed living. Yet, the fact that my dad can't go there with me anymore does not mean that he can't still go fishing with me. It just means that we have to find other places to fish. We have to approach the rivers with a different set of priorities.

Just as Descartes notes the cognitive limits on human thought, there are also limits that accompany our particular mode of embodiment. Some mountain grades are too steep for humans, but just right for

31

goats. Some summits are inaccessible for humans, but easy nesting grounds for eagles. My dad's neuropathy is now a limiting factor in our fishing trips, but this is not something to see as an absolute and singular defeat, for when were we *not* limited in some respect by our embodiment?

There is a spot just a few hundred yards from that magical place on the Hiwassee where the mountainside just falls straight away from the road down to the river and it is inaccessible except by going into the river upstream and then floating down to it. And yet just as you can't get down to the river at that point, you also can't get back up to the trail there either. The steep grade signals impossibility in both directions. The only option is to keep going downstream in order to find a place to get back on the land.

No matter how healthy or strong I am, that slope to the river is one that forces me to adjust my plans and keep walking upstream. I do wish in many ways that my dad didn't have neuropathy. I wish in other ways that he were still 65 instead of 80. However, this is where we are. This is the particular location on the lived trajectory where he and I have to learn to read the rest of the vista that lies in front of us. We could decide that our fishing days are basically over. Or, we could find ways to see the changes necessitated by his condition as goads to facilitate becoming open to new ways of seeing the rivers and finding novel ways to navigate their terrain. I hope we have the strength and courage to do the latter, but it is a constant challenge.

Becoming sometimes sucks because it is never stable. The goal, it turns out, was never to catch a bunch of fish and leave on a high note, like George Costanza walking out of the room on a laugh. The goal has always been to find ways to keep fishing. We have to learn how to stay in the conversation even after the laughter fades.

But here is the cool thing. My dad can't go with me to that spot on the Hiwassee anymore, but my son, Atticus, can. And I take him there because I know about it from the times with my dad. It is because my dad and I explored together that I can now open those spaces for my son to explore. And, since empirical aloneness is not ethical aloneness, every time I am there (whether by myself or with my son), I am there with my dad. The relational potential continues even when the society fades. It is because we are defined by life together, as Dietrich Bonhoeffer would say, that we can hike and fish by ourselves and yet never really be alone.

In the end, vulnerability and relational potentiality always remain intertwined even if revealed in different degrees at different times. Kierkegaard comments that while standing there by the sea at Gilbjerget, he realized something important:

> I stood there alone and forsaken and the power of the sea and the battle of the elements reminded me of my nothingness, while the sure flight of the birds reminded me on the other hand of Christ's words, 'Not a sparrow will fall to the earth without your heavenly Father's will'. (35 I A 68; as cited in Kierkegaard 1996, p. 27)

He then explains that this joint awareness hit him so profoundly that, as he puts it, "I felt at one how great and yet how insignificant I am. These two great forces, pride and humility, amicably combined. Fortunate the [person] for whom *this* is possible every moment of his life" (35 I A 68; as cited in Kierkegaard 1996, p. 27).

Fortunate is that person indeed.

Thoreau went to the woods to live deliberately.
Socrates left the cave to live truthfully.
Kierkegaard went to the sea to live reflectively.
Nietzsche went to the mountains to live willfully.

But whether by an out-and-back trail, or on a loop, they all then came back to the trailhead.

Thoreau made his way back to Emerson's house because it was time to get dinner.
Socrates stayed in Athens and obeyed the laws as an example of what virtue requires.
Kierkegaard returned to school and completed his studies.
Nietzsche's Zarathustra eventually had to come down from the mountains to find an audience.

The culture of success tells us that the fishing trip was good because we caught fish.

Alternatively, faithfulness reminds us that life is more joyful when we keep going fishing.

On a different hike, Kierkegaard recounts walking through the woods by Lake Gurre. He notes that "the forest itself is fairly large and wild, and only the track (not a road) reminds us that we still have any connection with the human world" (35 I A 64; as cited in Kierkegaard 1996, p. 25). Even though we eventually have to stop hiking because it gets too dark or cold, or we have to stop fishing particular spots because we get too old and our legs give out due to a physical condition, the question continues: "what will we do with our finitude?"

Will we stop fishing just because we can't fish *that* spot?
Will we stop hiking just because we don't have time to go to a new trail?

The constancy of faithful becoming doesn't eschew the joy of being where we are; it facilitates it.

Kierkegaard knows he will have to return to the towns soon, but there, at that moment, "when this landscape is viewed in the afternoon light and the sun is still high enough to give the necessary sharp contours to the friendly landscape, like a melodious voice that is accented sharply enough not to lisp, our entire surroundings seem to whisper to us, 'This is a good place to be'" (35 I A 64; as cited in Kierkegaard 1996, pp. 24-25).

There it is.
Here we are.
Can we, with Kierkegaard say, "This is a good place to be"?

I hope so.

Whether on the mountaintop looking down at the river below or in the valley looking up from the middle of the river, we are where we are. Anne Lamott encourages us to "be where our feet are," but it is crucial to realize that cultivating faithfulness as a way of life means that we are not stuck. Movement remains possible because we are who we are becoming.

Keep hiking.
Keep fishing.
Remember the blessed moments by yourself and with others.
Be alone but remember your relational location.

Trails, like rivers, are never the same for long.
You are always embodied so adjust as necessary.

3

On Being Known

Sometimes we get to the mountains, but other times we are stuck in bed surrounded by tissues and decongestant. We would be wrong to think that going camping with Kierkegaard is something that only happens when we are feeling good.

I once had a professor of comparative literature in graduate school who would say that when he got sick, he would "go to bed with Jane Austen." Of course, he would then laugh out loud—the sort of big belly laugh that always made me think that he would be a good candidate for the department store Santa Claus—and go on to explain that Austen was the author who spoke most directly to his soul in its moments of exposed misery. Her writings allowed his being confined to bed with a runny nose and fever to be a little less bad because he was reminded that he always navigated the human condition with others.

Notice the duality, yet again, of vulnerability and relationality.

While admitting that few folks would want to take an existentialist philosopher with them to the campsite, I always found his claim to be bizarre because there are not many thinkers that I find less compelling when it comes to the human condition than Jane Austen. My wife would disagree with me on this, but I think it just due to her current, and quite unfortunate, infatuation with *Bridgerton* on Netflix (gross). In all seriousness, though, I never liked Austen because her books tend to be defined by the sort of longing and despair that gets resolved by external achievements (in her case, typically marriage). From where I stand, what is most interesting and troubling about life doesn't work that way. The deepest longings are not ones that can be satisfied by obtaining a particular object. The worst despair is not overcome by a change in possessions or by updating one's relational status on social media. So, if my former professor went to bed with Jane Austen in the same way that I go to bed every night listening to reruns of *Frasier*, then I get it—it allows us to shut down the reflective engine of our mind that haunts our waking hours. If, however, he means that Austen is where we should turn when we are faced with our own weakness, then I think there are better options.

Where should we turn when we are overwhelmed by the heaviness of life itself? As my grandmother asked once, what do we do when we are just too tired to go to heaven? I am sure that I don't have great answers to such questions and I am also sure that whatever hunches I have are likely to fall as flat for many of you as my former professor's endorsement of Austen does for me. Hope remains, though, that sometimes we are benefited from the realization that others are struggling in the same ways that we are, even if we then turn to different places to work through the difficulties.

When I am faced with the weighty realities of human life, I watch reruns of *Cheers* (which is an amazing show, but not as good as *Frasier*, though better than *Wings*, which is still really good), because the theme song simply gets everything right:

Making your way in the world today
Takes everything you've got
Taking a break from all your worries

Sure would help a lot
Wouldn't you like to get away? . . .

Sometimes you want to go
Where everybody knows your name
And they're always glad you came
You want to be where you can see
Our troubles are all the same
You want to be where everybody knows your name.[3]

When I hear this, my soul just cries out "Amen!" Yes, I want to get away from my worries and the exhaustion of continuing to put one foot in front of the other and trying to smile at people while doing it. I *do* want to be where everyone knows my name and where our troubles are all the same. These famous lyrics are deeper than they might initially seem. They speak to the idea of *being known*.

What these lyrics get right is that who we are, most deeply, is not something that can be encapsulated into easily consumed narratives. This is the case for the same reason that a 10-mile hike or a 20-mile mtn bike ride can't be reduced to the pictures that we post once we get back home. Lived experience is excessive. Those who truly "know" us understand that there is always more to know. They do not reduce us to the ideas that they have of us. They do not fit us into the mold that serves their purposes. Our troubles are all the same, as the song says, not in terms of specifics, but in relation to the way that all of our particular circumstances are made meaningful by what we share: our embodiment, our finitude, our hopes, and our awareness of the reality of loss.

What the Cheers song understands about the human condition can also be found in easily one of the best movies of all time, *Tombstone*.[4]

---

3   By Gary Portnoy and Judy Hart-Angelo, single originally released in 1983; later appeared in an expanded version on Portnoy's 2004 album, "Keeper."
4   Kevin Jarre, *Tombstone*, original script, 1993, available at: https://www.daily script.com/scripts/tombstone.pdf

Consider that scene where Doc Holiday is in a hospital bed and has a conversation with Wyatt Earp. Earp asks him, "How we feeling today, Doc?" to which Holiday replies, "I'm dying; how are you?" Earp then says, "Pretty much the same." I love that this line passes so quickly without much fanfare in the film. The double entendre hangs in the air for all who would care to consider it: Is Earp saying that he is "pretty much the same" as he usually is? Or is he saying that he is "pretty much the same" as Holiday in that he too is dying, but maybe not in as pressing a sense? That the film allows these two options to go unresolved is impressive, because normally Hollywood is not known for being existentially nuanced.

"Pretty much the same." That about sums it up. "Our troubles," as the Cheers song notes, are similar because they are the ones that accompany the human condition.

We need to be careful here, though. It is tempting to stress the realities of the human condition in ways that cause us to overlook the singularity of individual lives. Even if "our troubles are all the same," that doesn't mean that my relationship to such troubles is simply interchangeable with yours. Crucially, and without exception, we all have to navigate the realities of our shared human condition for ourselves. This doesn't mean that we don't lean heavy into relationships and communities of trust—remember we want to go where everybody knows our name, which means that we always remain defined at our core by the quality of "being-with-others." Even in community, we still have to figure out, with Lamott, how to "be where our feet are," and that is a singular task.

Martin Heidegger (2010) expresses well this idea of the singularity of existence when he talks about the quality of "mineness" that accompanies all experience and meaning making. Although his specific account is embedded in technical Husserlian phenomenology, the basic idea is that our experience of the world is always *ours*.

Even though the singer Everlast might be right to say that we would see things differently if we could "walk a mile in their shoes," when it comes to embodied existence, we can't ever take *our* "shoes" off. Conscious experience is always subjectively located.

As Thomas Nagel (1979) provocatively puts it, there is no way for a human being to know what it is like to be a bat. We can put on a bat costume and hang upside down in a cave, but all we would ever know is what it is like for a human being to try to act like a bat. Heidegger pushes this point further by saying that we wouldn't even know what it is like for a "human being" in general to do this, but only what it is like for *this particular* human being, that is, *me*, to do so.

Now, before you jump to extremes and decide that this is just a slippery slope to incoherent subjectivism, slow down and pay attention to what all these thinkers are indicating: lived experience is not abstract; it is personal; it is mine. As such, the idea of "being-known" is not an abstract idea of knowing about the concept of "humanity," or what Karl Marx (1978) would term "species-being." Instead, it is a concrete reality of being invested in and sharing with another. As my wife and I said in our wedding vows: "Come let's walk together and talk along the way." Being known is about walking with someone who walks with you. It is not just a matter of sharing similar troubles, but of helping each other better to carry the burden that only they can lift.

This might be a frustrating realization. Far too often we act like we can carry each other's burdens. That might be right for Jane Austen novels, but it is existentially false. Given the mineness of experience, I can't navigate the human condition, even if shared, for another. All I can do is to try to help them to navigate it better for themselves. But this doesn't entail some sort of "conservative" claptrap about picking yourself up by your own bootstraps. Part of how we facilitate others being able to navigate their own existential situation more effectively is by working for structures of social justice that do not add unnecessary weights to the existential baggage we unavoidably carry.

Whether our social vision is progressive or conservative, we are all faced with the necessity of deciding who it is that we want to become, given who it is that we have been made. We can lean on others, but we can't ride their existential coattails the way that Marty McFly would hitch a ride with his skateboard by grabbing on the back bumper of a car. We can facilitate the freedom of others, but we can't make them free by taking away their agency.

Heidegger (2010) puts it this way: we can *leap-in* for others or *leap-ahead* of them, and the difference is crucial. Leaping-in is a matter of doing something for someone that hands them a finished product, something requiring no more effort on their part. I always think of the parent who just does their child's science fair project and then gives it to the kid and says, "Here you go." Although such parents might think they are helping the child, all that they are really doing is preventing the child from becoming the person who has done the work. In effect, the parent has eliminated the child's agency by taking away the precious freedom required to navigate the challenge. Leaping-ahead is by contrast akin to the parent who tells their child that they are going to stay up with them all night long and help them work on the project, but then waits patiently on the child to take the steps at the right times to move forward. Whereas leaping-in strips away freedom, leaping-ahead facilitates it.

When it comes to being-known, only leaping-ahead makes such knowledge possible. Going where everybody knows your name means that you are irreplaceably recognized. You are not interchangeable with all the others, just a face in the crowd like any other face.

Every other is absolutely significant in their own way, even though everyone is also defined by the shared condition of embodied finitude. When Jacques Derrida (1995) cryptically writes that "*tout autre est tout autre*" ("every other is absolutely other"), this is really what he is getting at. We are all, every single one of us, *ourselves*. And yet, as myself, I know you only insofar as I realize that you, like me, are yourself in radically singular ways. Part of the shared condition which allows that our "troubles are all the same" is the fact that we are all inescapably, irreplaceably who we are. That then presents us with the issue of facing up to who it is that we are becoming. Our selfhood is to a significant degree a decision to move in the direction of those who encourage us toward virtue.

Being known is, thus, fundamentally about willing ourselves into relationships that are life-giving. When we walk with others—whether up mountains or through valleys—we are actively invested in becoming the person that walking with them is likely to make us.

Here, I believe, that moving conversation between Doc Holiday and Wyatt Earp continues to speak to us. As Earp ignores Holiday's protestations against playing a hand of cards, Holiday says:

> You are the most fallible, stubborn, self-deluded, bull-headed man I have ever known in my entire life. Yet with all, you are the only human being in my entire life ever gave me hope.

Then, after recounting a story about the only woman he ever loved, Holiday asks Earp: "What do you want, Wyatt?" To which Earp responds, "just to live a normal life." Holiday, ever the existentialist philosopher replies, "there's no normal life, Wyatt, there's just life . . . so get on with it."

We might think that Holiday is being a bit cold and callous. I mean, Wyatt is there by his bedside out of love, after all. But, my own reading of this scene is that Holiday is modeling what leaping-ahead of looks like. He is explaining to Wyatt that the best way that he can show his friendship is to go live his life and do so on purpose. Holiday is the sort of person who continues to help his friend become (that is, live into faithfulness), rather than being content with who he is (that is, succumbing to the allure of success). In this way, being-known is actually quite rare—hence the soul-cry in the *Cheers* theme song for a place where we are known. We long for what we lack. In a time of maximal connections via social networks, we are so often, and so very deeply, profoundly lonely.

At the end of this hospital bed scene, Holiday looks at a little novella that Wyatt has handed him; it is a short story entitled, "My Friend, Doc Holiday." Now this might seem insignificant, but it is depending on an earlier scene from the film where Holiday, whose illness is clearly progressing, is told by another member of the group "Doc, you ought to be in bed. What the hell are you doing this for, anyway?" Holiday turns and says, "Wyatt Earp is my friend." In exasperation, the other man replies, "Hell, I got lots of friends." And Holiday simply notes, "I don't."

In that two word sentence we see why it matters so much that Earp calls Holiday his "friend" on that booklet. It stands as a testament to the fact that Holiday has lived into the person he had hoped to become: Wyatt's friend. Wyatt knows Holiday's name: *my friend*.

We all long to be where everybody knows our name. The question is by what name will we be known? Who are we becoming?

The really scary part is that we always are who we are becoming. Aristotle understands this in his idea of virtue ethics. He rightly recognized that a person's character is formed by habits. What we do without explicitly thinking about it is reflective of who we are most deeply. So, what we are making ordinary today is what will be implicit for us tomorrow. What we make as the result of conscious decision today will be the background assumption for our decisions later.

Nietzsche says that we must *become who we are*, but I think it is the opposite: we must own up to the fact that *we are who we are becoming*.

If you don't like who you are, then you definitely won't like who you are becoming.

So change things.
Right now.
Habit takes time to break and time to form.
Finitude is real, don't waste time.

Perhaps one of the most famous repeating motifs on *Cheers* was the way that the character, Norm, was greeted every time he walked in the bar. "NORM!" everyone would yell. They all knew his name. But, perhaps tragically, despite all that we see his character do and go through over the years of the show, he never really changes in any significant sense. He is on the first episode who he would be/become on the last one. Indeed, the final episode explicitly stresses this fact.

In their final conversation with Sam—who has just returned from yet another an ill-fated reconnection with Diane—the other characters (Norm, Frasier, Carla, Cliff, and Woody) are all smoking cigars and having a beer together when Sam asks, "What is the point to life?"[5] Here, we are met with a moment of existential awareness in the midst of sitcom trivialities. Cliff initially offers the suggestion that the point of life is "comfortable shoes." They surmise that Aristotle was likely such a great thinker because of his sandals. Then, Carla chimes in to suggest that "having kids" is the point of life. Frasier joins the conversation by displaying the intellectual erudition for which his Harvard education has prepared him. His contention is that some might say life is just absurd and without meaning at all. His nihilistic alternative is quickly undercut by Woody's proclamation that Dr. Crane is just "trying to keep the conversation lively," and then the young bartender notes that his life has been significant due to his relationships with the folks there at the bar.

Ironically, given our reflections here about the significance of naming and being-known, Woody expresses his appreciation that none

---

5   *Cheers*, "One for the Road," original script, 1993, available at:
https://tvshowtranscripts.ourboard.org/viewtopic.php?f=849&t=23611

of them call him "Huckleberry." When Norm asks if that's his "nickname" back in Hanover, Indiana (where he is famously from), Woody says, "no, Woody is." Thus, he repeats the Derridean point that no matter how well you know another person, they can never be completely known—they always remain, to some degree, elusive, no matter how hard we try to grasp them. This is what Emmanuel Levinas (1969) terms their "absolute alterity." Though Woody's comment is funnier than anything Levinas ever says on the matter, the point is quite similar: knowing another is about *continuing* to get to know them. The investment in friendship is a matter of faithfulness.

As they all leave, Norm hangs back for a minute and gives his idea of the point of life. In a short monologue that might fit well in Plato's *Symposium*, he contends that the most important thing in life is love. He then comments, "You want to know what I love?" To which Sam quite predicably responds, "Beer, Norm?" The entire audience is now expecting Norm to reply with an affirmation that Sam's supposition is correct. But, instead, Norm looks at his watch and says, "Yeah, I've have a quick one." In that moment, he was, is, and forever will be, the Norm we have all come to "know" and to love. As the laughter of the audience dies down Norm continues on to finish his thoughts about the point of life: "I love that (bar)stool. If there is a heaven, I don't want to go there unless that stool is waiting for me . . . and I'll tell ya what, even God better not be on it."

Here we are at the end of the eleven-year run of the show, and yet Norm is right where we met him in the first episode: drinking beer and loving his stool. He is a man of remarkable consistency, and apparently he is quite easy to satisfy. But, consistency doesn't preclude profundity. As he prepares to leave the bar, Norm tells Sam that he knew Sam would come back from his attempt to leave with Diane. Met with Sam's incredulous reply, Norm explains that, "You can never be unfaithful to your one true love." "You always come back to her," he concludes.

St. Augustine claims that we are defined by what we love. Maybe that is a good way to understand how habit works for Aristotle. Habit translates love into practice.

Socrates loved inquiry. Norm loved his stool. My former professor loved Jane Austen. We know their names, but who knows ours?

When we are too sick to get on the trails, you can go to bed with Jane Austen, but I will just keep watching *Cheers*.

4

Lilies, Birds, and Vanessa

Prior to the COVID pandemic, my wife and I had only been camping together one time. It was our first date. Things did not go as I had planned.

In order to understand what a mess that first camping trip was, it is important to get a little back-story on our relationship.

I first met Vanessa when we were both 16 years old. Her family had recently started coming to our church and so we met in the youth group on Wednesday nights. At the time, I was dating another girl, let's call her Lauren. Lauren and Vanessa quickly became friends and so Lauren, Vanessa, and I would sit together at church and go to "afterglows" on Sunday evenings after church, which was basically just a sexy name for going out to eat.

My best friend throughout my childhood and teen years was a guy we will call Brian. Brian and I had grown up together and were like brothers. He and I both even had matching pairs of shorts when I was a kid that had been made from his grandmother's old drapes. Well, Brian had not been coming to my church very regularly for various reasons, but he decided to start coming again. The first event he came to was a youth group skating party. He and I went together and of course I introduced him to Lauren and Vanessa, who were hanging together at the event. Later that evening, Vanessa came up to me while Brian was somewhere else and said, "I want your friend!" So, I told her that maybe the four of us could plan to go get some food or something. We did. From then on, Brian and Vanessa were inseparable, and they dated for four years, and by contrast, Lauren and I didn't make it for many months after the skating party. Brian eventually became my college roommate and our relationship continued on as strong as ever. Then, as is often the case in college, fraternities create "brothers" by ending old friendships. Brian and I had a bit of a falling out, he moved out of our dorm, and soon afterwards he and Vanessa broke up. She was devastated and claimed that since I had been there from the beginning of their relationship, I was the "only one who understood her pain." That was obviously false, but I didn't mind much since I liked hanging out with her and, given that we had been friends for years, she filled some of the gap in my own life that had been created when Brian replaced me with his new "brothers."

For the next couple of years, Vanessa spent an enormous amount of time at my house. I had moved back in with my parents to save money during my last couple years in college. My brother wrote most of her papers for her English classes, I did most of her math homework, and my family more or less adopted her—which worked out great for my sister who had grown tired of being surrounded by three brothers and so having Vanessa as a "sister" really was great for her during her teen years. Although I imagine you might not believe me, through all this time, it never even occurred to me to see Vanessa in a romantic way. She was my friend, and we became extremely close, but she dated other people, I dated other people, and our friendship was simply a consistent backdrop. Ah, but a funny thing then happened on the way to Sadie Hawkins at Lee University.

Sadie Hawkins is a famous function at Lee. It happens every Fall semester and was an outdoor event at a farm near campus where there would be fire-pits, live music, good food, and generally it had a collegiate fall festival sort of vibe. The wrinkle was that it was a "girls ask guys" event, which is what passed as "progressive" at our Christian college that to this day still has mandatory chapel every week and curfews for the on-campus students. Well, Vanessa had been expressing interest in a dude I knew and liked, but thought was kind of a doofus embodying a classic all smile no substance combination. So, one evening, Vanessa and I were sitting outside on the porch of her townhouse off campus, hence no curfew, and I inquired as to whether she was going to ask that guy to Sadie Hawkins. She said, "No, I kinda like someone else." Clueless, I replied, "What?! Who do you like now?" She coyly looked away without saying anything, but kind of smirked in the process.

Well, to make a long story shorter, we ended up kissing that night and got married three years later. We have now been married 22 years.

With that background in place, you should know that in all the time Vanessa and I had spent together over the years, we did not share much time in the outdoors. She was an only child, had generally been spoiled by her parents, and though not growing up in any extravagance, I used to refer to her as a "Tampa Palms Rich Kid," referring to the large and famous subdivision where she lived during high school. I should also note that so you won't think I was being rude to her, she had long referred to me as "96 years old" because, being the oldest of four kids, I had an over-developed sense of maturity and responsibility, or so she claimed. Vanessa used to say that she "does not sweat, but merely glistens." Ugh, right? So, the mere idea of being in the woods and sleeping on the ground in a tent just sounded to her like textbook misery.

In fact, the only time I can remember even being in the mountains with her was while she was still dating Brian. I was with some other girl at the time. We hiked up Chilhowee Mountain in Tennessee and were at this place called "The Rock" on top of the mountain,

49

which was a popular place to go watch the sunset. After the sun went down, we stayed a bit longer to see the stars come out. When we finally decided to head back to the truck, we walked into the tree-cover and immediately realized we were in a mess. No flashlights, no visibility. We ended up using our Indiglo watches, which if you're old enough, you may recall as the coolest thing ever because they glowed green with a push of a button, to get just enough light to make our way down the mountain and avoid the numerous cliffs that ran parallel to our path.

That night on Chilhowee mountain was part of our shared history. And so as we began seeing each other in a new, romantic, way, I suggested that our first real date should be to go camping.

Bad idea.

To her credit, she knew how much I loved camping and thought it sounded like a cool idea and so we packed our stuff and headed up to Fall Creek Falls campground in Tennessee. It was late autumn and quite chilly, but not actually cold. Accordingly, I checked the weather and brought what I thought were appropriately rated sleeping bags and other gear. But I failed to check the weather for where we were going, which was a much higher elevation than where I lived, and so it came as quite a surprise that night when it dropped down to 12 degrees (Fahrenheit).

The Tampa Palms Rich Kid was neither comfortable nor happy.

All the water I brought froze solid. Our eggs for breakfast were frozen. Our sleeping bags were nowhere near warm enough, so it was a miserable and very long night. The only thing that made it passable was that, since it was our first real date, our spirts were high and we both tried to find it funny—which is hard when you are really cold. Shivering is not the same thing as shaking from laughter.

Like our approach to having children, that camping trip was a "one and done" endeavor. Vanessa quickly warmed up to our relationship, regained a sense of comfort, and informed me that even though she loved me, she was fine never going camping again.

I soon discovered it wasn't just the cold. She truly hates snakes, spiders, and ticks. She is scared of bears and sleeping in shelters without monitored alarm systems. Even when she now comes with me off-roading in my truck, which is only a very occasional outing and when it is absolutely required to get to a hiking spot, she consistently asks: "So, you keep claiming that people do this on purpose. Why? Is it supposed to be fun?"

The point is that camping has until very recently represented for Vanessa a series of difficulties that lead to worry, rather than to the relaxation that motivates my own trips to the mountains.

The pandemic has changed things because it coincided with our son being old enough really to enjoy spending time in the outdoors, and since we couldn't safely be around other people, we started hiking, kayaking, and camping together in order to make the time more bearable. Nonetheless, Vanessa still doesn't love camping, and although she does enjoy kayaking and paddleboarding on flat water, she greatly prefers lying on a beach to hiking in the mountains. When we are camping, she often suggests that we just go out and do everything one does while camping, from building a fire to making dinner, and then just come home before going to sleep. Sleeping in a tent remains anxiety inducing to her. For my part, I never sleep so well as when I am on my ExPed10 sleeping mat and take the rainfly off the tent so that I can see the stars. Opposites attract, I guess.

The point of telling this admittedly elaborate story is to highlight the fact that often the very thing that brings peace and joy to one person is the source of fear and anxiety for another.

None of us is free of worry. Regardless of what the cause of that worry is, we are all plagued by a realization of the tragedies that accompany the vulnerability essential to our shared human condition. My attempt to bring peace and joy into my family by suggesting that we spend a few days in the mountains is never received that way by my wife. She often responds, "Can't we find a cabin somewhere that is still in the mountains, but has real beds . . . and doors?"

Whether it is camping, or reading, or napping, or sitting on a beach, we all find ways to navigate the stress of existence.

One of the problematic tendencies of such strategies, however, is that we act like we need to *go somewhere else* in order to get away from what defines our *here and now*. Such episodic escapism is fine. We all need vacations. The goal of "getting away," though, should be to find a way *faithfully* to navigate our daily lives so that they are not defined by worry, but by peace; not by despair, but by hope; not by stress, but by gratitude.

My wife's beach preferences notwithstanding, I think we can learn a lot about finding joy by paying attention to things in the mountains: The song of the birds and the roar of the waterfall pierce the underlying silence; the seemingly gravity defying ability of trees that grow out from the side of rocky cliffs; the process of restoration that accompanies the falling of leaves and their return a few months later; the feeling of sublime grandeur when confronted by a vista that extends for miles. All of these are not just occasions for reflection, but invitations for intentional growth. We just need to develop the eyes to see and the ears to hear. Worry gets in the way of paying attention. Paying attention fights worry because it opens onto an infinity hidden in plain sight among the downed leaves and ice-tinged rivers.

In order to think a bit more about how the mountains help us to overcome our human, all too human, tendency to worry, I will turn to Kierkegaard's series of *Upbuilding Discourses* where he reflects on Matthew 6 about the lilies of the field and birds of the air.

Let's get the Biblical passage in front of us so that we can better follow Kierkegaard's analysis of it:

> Therefore I tell you, do not worry about your life, what you will eat or drink; or about your body, what you will wear. Is not life more than food, and the body more than clothes? Look at the birds of the air; they do not sow or reap or store away in barns, and yet your heavenly Father feeds them. Are you not much more valuable than they? Can any one of you by worrying add a single hour to your life? And why do you worry about clothes? See how the flowers of the field grow. They do not labor or spin. Yet I tell you that not even Solomon in all his splendor was dressed like one of these. If that is how God clothes the grass of the field, which is here today and tomorrow is thrown into the fire, will he not much more clothe you—you of little faith? So do not worry, saying, 'What shall we eat?' or 'What shall we drink?' or 'What shall we wear?' For the pagans run after all these things, and your heavenly Father knows that you need them. But seek first his kingdom and his righteousness, and all these things will be given to you as well. Therefore do not worry about tomorrow, for tomorrow will worry about itself. Each day has enough trouble of its own. (Matthew 6: 25-34, NIV).

"Do not worry about tomorrow." Easier said than done! But, notice, that this command is preceded with "therefore."

Indicator word!
Argument alert!

What is the argument that invites the conclusion that we should not worry about tomorrow? Moreover, even if we followed the argument, this alone doesn't mean that we would be able to enact its conclusion in our lived realities. So, assuming that the argument is sound, to what teachers can we turn to learn how to live into its truth?

Following the Biblical author, Kierkegaard suggests that it is the lilies of the field and birds of the air who stand out as the proper instructors for our own human existence. In the "prayer" that opens one of his lily/bird discourses, he stresses that we need to turn to these natural teachers because it is when we are surrounded by people, rather than flowers and fowl, that we most easily forget what it means to be human.

Let's pray with Kierkegaard:

> Father in heaven, what we in company with people, especially in a crowd of people, come to know with difficulty, and what we, if we have come to know it somewhere else, so easily forget in company with people, especially in a crowd of people—what it is to be a human being and what religiously is the requirement for being a human being—would that we might learn it or, if it is forgotten, that we might learn it again from the lily and the bird; would that we might learn it, if not all at once, then at least some of it, and little by little; would that from the lily and the bird we might this time learn silence, obedience, joy! (Kierkegaard 1997, p. 3).

In light of my suggestion that ethical aloneness is impossible for relational beings like us, it might seem odd that Kierkegaard locates other people as the source of difficulty for our awareness, and the cause of forgetfulness of everything essential. When we press in a bit, though, the oddness disappears. Kierkegaard, like Nietzsche, Emerson, Thoreau, Heidegger, Sartre, and Beauvoir, among many other existentially oriented thinkers, is warning against the ways that social narratives so often become normative for our self-identity.

Rather than being defined by what ought to be deepest in us, we are defined largely by what other people say. As we saw with the Cheers theme, being known is never about being reducible to sameness, but standing singularly amidst the solidarity of the human condition. The temptation to being "named" by others is significant, though, no matter how much existentialism we read. We all are seduced to some degree by fitting in with the "cool kids." Indeed, think about how often we refer to what "they" think as normative for what we should do.

Kierkegaard's reference to the "religious" requirements for being human speaks to this depth that we so often make shallow via social media as we try to fit in with "influencer culture"—which often is just a different face for the same "asshole" dynamics that we considered earlier. It is worth saying again that we can understand religion in very specific, confessional ways, but also more broadly as a matter of our deepest commitments that are determinate of who we take ourselves to be and who it is that we hope to become. That is, religious requirements speak to the locus of our faith and the direction of our lived risk.

In his understanding of religious requirements as pressing upon us despite the siren song of "the they," Kierkegaard is on to something important. I often tell my students that the only real downside to going on study-away trips for an extended period, like a semester-long excursion, rather than just the spring break trip, is that when they return, everything that seemed to matter most about their social context at the university will seem trivial and almost farcical. In my own case, I spent a semester studying in Cambridge, UK when I was in college. It was an amazing time, but like a multiday backpacking trip, the span of four months away was long enough to reset the pacing of my existence. Importantly, when we shift our pace and change our bodily engagement, it adjusts what we hold to be true. We don't just "hold" beliefs like we hold a phone or a rock, but instead we enact them with the lived priorities of our embodiment. As is the case anytime I go to the mountains, things were slower in Cambridge. I had time to sit and think, or to go for a walk, or to a pub with friends.

The point is that I *felt* like I had time.

Time was ample. It was no longer defined by its fleeting character. My lived existence no longer presented itself according to a logic of scarcity, but instead according to a logic of plentitude. Time in Cambridge was for making meaning, not just meeting deadlines.

Then I returned to my own hectic campus.

Instantly, I was out of step with the pacing and priorities of my peers. I just didn't care as much about the fraternity party, or who so and so was dating, or what internship deadline was approaching. But then, as I adjusted back to the college context, I also slipped back into what "they" said was important and what "they" said was stressful. Soon, I was also caught back up in the things that my Cambridge-self would have ignored as unimportant. I was overwhelmed by the deadlines, stressed by the social pressures, and no longer viewed time as a resource, but a terrible master.

My experience was akin to that of Kierkegaard's. When we are most surrounded by others, we forget what it means to be a self. That's the basic reason that empirical aloneness allows us to remember the value of relational existence. The crowd has its own logic, but it is not a logic that works well when in the mountains.

Speed, accomplishment, pressure, money, and ego are not values that are shared by the lilies and birds. Just as my Cambridge-self found the social realities of my college life to be out of step with what matters most deeply, the lilies and the birds quietly scorn the stressors that the crowd takes to be so very important.

Kierkegaard refers to the lily and the bird as "silent teachers" because they do not speak in the words that our fellow human beings, our social peers, use. Instead, they require us to grow silent in order to hear the lesson (Kierkegaard 1997, p. 10).

What is that lesson learned in silence? It is the one we have been discussing throughout this book: the importance of becoming humble in order to stand in confidence.

Kierkegaard puts it this way: What are we to do to "seek first the kingdom of God"? His answer is that, "in a certain sense it is nothing. In the deepest sense you shall make yourself nothing, become nothing before God, learn to be silent" (Kierkegaard 1997, pp. 10-11). Becoming nothing and becoming silent . . . these are the keys to God's kingdom. So long as we think we have it figured out, and proclaim our wisdom to all who would listen, we fail to appreciate that in our egoistic bombast we are fools merely babbling about how smart our babble is. So long as we position ourselves in the crowd—and understand ourselves according to its external logic of success and comparison—we will fail to realize that "the advantage of the human being over the animal is the ability to speak, but, in relation to God, wanting to speak can easily become the corruption of the human being. . . . God is infinite wisdom; what the human being knows is idle chatter. . . . Only in much fear and trembling is a human being able to speak with God" (Kierkegaard 1997, p. 11).

The lily and the bird understand that there is nothing to say, but much to learn.

In their very silence they teach us to become silent, to cultivate the habit of listening. Prayer, then, becomes a matter of learning to listen. We must become like the person who "learned" that "to pray is not to listen to oneself speak but is to become silent and to remain silent, to wait until the one praying hears God" (Kierkegaard 1997, p. 12). According to the logic of the crowd, it is the one who speaks most who gains the most ground. The people that the crowd labels "successful" are those who have the most to say to the rest of us about how we should live. The lily and the bird know differently. They appreciate that the one who speaks most is probably the one who is most fearful of what they might learn in silence. Learning silence ruptures the narrative of self-importance that characterizes the speech of those who garner large audiences.

In contrast to the motivational speaker, the college administrator, the wall-street banker, and the politician, who reinforce their status through facilitating the distraction of hurry, "the bird is silent and waits" (Kierkegaard 1997, p. 13).

Learning to become silent is hard enough, but learning to wait is harder still.

For whom or for what do we wait?

Kierkegaard's answer is simple enough: *we wait for God*. Perhaps this sounds too religious for some of you. I get it. This sort of view can quickly be confused with the nonsense that one hears now from so many white Evangelicals in America. In such contexts, "waiting on God" becomes not much more than a justification for inaction, for complacency, for abdicating our ethical responsibility in the face of the widow, the orphan, and the stranger. It ends up being not an expression of humility, hospitality, and gratitude in the face of excess, mystery, and vulnerability, but instead an appeal to divine sanction for the crowd's behavior. For Kierkegaard, however, the appeal to God is offered as a reminder of our human perspectival location. We are existing, and therefore can't get out of existence to understand it. Waiting on God means that we live into our limitations. When we wait, we are cognizant of the fact that we are dependent. Waiting challenges all of our pretentions to self-sufficiency.

If we really were as powerful as we claim to be, we would never have to wait.

Indeed, think of how we narrate time in relation to social status. The famous actor, athlete, or businessperson is too important to be "kept waiting." Yet, the immigrant, the poor, the marginalized, and the disabled are made to get used to waiting as the condition of their existence itself. In relation to God, however, we are *all* made to wait. There is no VIP line like there is at the airport, the club, or the hotel. We all stand together.

And as we wait, we learn to become silent as we realize that our speech will not get us to the front of the line. Sexy words that shorten the waiting do not matter to the lily and the bird because they understand that there is no reason to be in a hurry. As we become like the lily and the bird, we become "nothing" as the condition of becoming ourselves.

Becoming nothing is not a matter of nihilistic insignificance, but of appropriate self-awareness.

Kierkegaard is not Kafka.

Listen to Kierkegaard's account of name and naming:

> Would that you in silence might forget yourself, what you yourself are called, your own name, the famous name, the wretched name, the insignificant name, in order in silence to pray to God: "Hallowed be *your* name!" Would that in silence you might forget yourself, your plans, the great, all encompassing plans, or the limited plans for your life and its future, in order in silence to pray to God: "*Your* kingdom come!" Would that in silence you might forget your will, your self-will, in order in silence to pray to God: "*Your* will be done!" Yes, if you could learn from the lily and the bird to become completely silent before God, in what then would the Gospel not be able to help you! Then nothing would be impossible for you. (Kierkegaard 1997, pp. 18-19)

I love that Kierkegaard highlights the absolute equality that exists before God. How crazy it would be to try to rank the importance of *this* bird as opposed to *that* one. What nonsense it would be to try to prioritize *this* lily over *that* one. Yet, alas, humans act like the judgment of the crowd can bestow such importance and justify such exclusion.

How many Instagram followers do *you* have?

How many people attend *your* church?
And, yes, facing up to the irony, how many people buy *your* book?

In relation to God, the lily and the bird teach us *all* that there is no hierarchy. The words of the powerful and the powerless equally reduce to idle chatter. The plans of the rich and the poor equally amount to nothing. The famous and the unknown are equally made to wait.

Pay attention, though, to the way that Kierkegaard then explains that this proclamation, "Hallowed be your name," is not an equalization in the name of something like a divine ego—as if God were the famous actor, the popular politician, or the rich businesswoman. Instead, God "gently and lovingly stoops down to the individual and whispers to him in order to attract him to the good" (Kierkegaard 1997, p. 19).

By focusing on God, instead of ourselves, we rightly gain self-understanding as we live into humility. Nothing is impossible "with God," because we no longer live according to the crowd's pacing and priorities. Seeking "first" the kingdom of God is a matter of realizing that our worries are misplaced accents on the deadlines that the birds and lilies ignore.

"Sometimes you want to go where everybody knows your name." The lilies and the birds teach us that in relation to God we are never nameless.

What I loved about Cambridge was that it allowed me to become invested, Kierkegaard's term is "earnest," in how I spent my time. I realized that I was able to decide otherwise than what my first intuition might be, which usually just reflected the old values of the crowd rather than allowing me to wait long enough to figure out my own.

What I love about camping is that it entirely interrupts the often forced pacing and priorities of my daily life. The point is that I get to embody a different speed. Setting up camp becomes a matter of facilitating the rest of the night. It focuses my energies on the fact that we are who we are becoming. Not spending time setting up camp appropriately can lead to a very long night of very little sleep. Making dinner becomes an event, whether by yourself or with others, because it is not something that you fit in among all the other deadlines ("Oh shoot, I guess I need to eat something"), but is the whole point of those minutes. Sitting by the fire is not just delaying something else, but reason enough to be.

But, when we lie down for the night, it is tempting to become anxious about all that remains to be done tomorrow.

The lesson from the lilies and the birds is that by focusing on what needs to be done today we are able to be free from worry because we are spending our time *living*. Becoming silent and learning to listen and wait translates into a rejection of the crowd's insistence that we get overwhelmed by what remains to be done. The lilies and the birds do what is needed, . . . and then do what is needed, . . . and then do what is needed. There is nothing artificial.

When camping, we can do the same. The lessons of the lilies and the birds are presented in large-print, as it were, when we are surrounded by the sound of crickets as we find ourselves out of range for notifications on our phone.

Alternatively, when surrounded by other people, especially in the crowd, we spend our time worrying about what we will need to do to impress "them." Stress is "named" as our normal state of affairs. So, we get used to things being this way and adjust to "fit in." Forgetting the invitation to learn silence, we grow accustomed to the sound of applause as the only feedback we desire. Rather than finding ourselves as always already "known" and "named" by God, we turn our attention to cultivating our "brand" so that others will care to learn our name.

It is often said that life is what happens while we were making other plans. In some sense, this is the basic insight of the lilies and the birds. The encouragement to stop worrying about tomorrow is not tantamount to willful blindness or indifference. It is, instead, a reminder that worry doesn't change anything for the better. The lilies do not hesitate to grow due to worry about the coming frost. They grow with an eye toward the sun that shines and the water that falls. They focus on where they are as the best strategy for becoming who they hope to be.

We might put it this way:
Birds build nests because that is what birds do.
Lilies grow because that is what lilies do.

Worrying about not being a good enough bird or not being a good enough lily is nonsense. They don't make plans to be birds or to be lilies and then put together a slide-deck with about strategy that concludes with a six-step action plan for how to be a better lily or bird and scale up this plan as they expand into new markets. Birds and lilies have no need for administrators, motivational speakers, or politicians because "success" is not something that gets defined for them by others. For the lily and the bird, success just *is* a faithful life.

Why is it so hard for humans to learn this lesson? Perhaps it's because we are stuck with an awareness of our finitude as a cause of worry, rather than the condition of action.

My wife doesn't like camping because she is worried about all that could happen while we are in the woods. As a result, we end up taking an enormous amount of stuff with us to the woods. My truck is packed full in awareness of every possible eventuality. Yes, it is always important to prepare before heading to the trails, but if we spend all our time trying to prepare for the trip, we can end up delaying our departure or not going at all. The lilies and the birds still prepare for tomorrow (nests are basically the bird's version of going to REI and getting the gear that is needed), but they do not *worry* about it. They realize that building the nest is what today requires. Tomorrow will require something else, so if we get overrun with worry about tomorrow, we will fail to get the gear today and therefore make tomorrow more of a mess.

Learning silence is crucial because it reminds us that doing more is usually not the answer. Doing less, becoming nothing, is not about throwing up our hands in quietist resignation, however. It is about being invested, earnest, and doing the best we can with what we have where we are. But, such activity must always undertaken with an awareness that our priorities and our pacing need to match.

Are we seeking what matters most because we know who we are? Or are we seeking the approval of "them" in order to feel like our hurry, our stress, and our exhaustion are justified?

I could have prepared better for that first camping trip with my wife (thankfully she married me anyway!), but once we were in the mountains, what good was it to worry about what I didn't bring? The best I could do is build a good fire, set up the tent, make dinner, and enjoy the time we had together. The same is true for every moment.

Yes, it can get cold. Yes, the water might freeze. Yes, the winds might blow down the tent or the nest. Yes, the snow might put out the fire and cover over the lilies. Alternatively the wildfire might burn the flowers and prevent us from making camp.

We must remember, though, that worrying about the wind doesn't make your nest stronger—only building a stronger nest does that. Worrying about the snow or the fire doesn't protect against such threats—but blooming where we are planted occasions joy here and now . . . come what may.

So, having learned silence from the lily and the bird, Kierkegaard then suggests that we learn obedience and ultimately joy.

That sounds good, doesn't it? Ultimately joy. Not joy . . . eventually. But, ultimately . . . joy.

Nearly 25 years ago I took my new girlfriend camping. Now we go camping all the time. The joy is not found in the camping, but in being together. I spent too many years frustrated that we were not camping together (annoyed that it got so cold that first night that, as the water froze, her worries were also solidified about being in the woods) that I forgot what mattered most.

The band Oasis gets the lesson of the lily and the bird right when they say, "be here, now."[6]

Yeah, that sounds right (both the song and also the message). So, with the lily and the bird, let's learn to move from silence, though obedience, and into joy . . . so that we can be ultimately, and faithfully, here, now.

---

6   Oasis, *Be Here, Now* (Creation Records, 1997).

5

The Joy Decision

The British punk/new wave band, Joy Division, has a song called "Love will Tear Us Apart."[7] The song is an attempt to narrate the difficulties of being in love when two people are moving in different directions. Whatever you might think of the band (for my money they are kinda *meh*), their song gets at an important aspect of Søren Kierkegaard's account of the lilies and the birds: the essential decision that attends the direction of our risk.

In a striking passage, Kierkegaard speaks of this decision that shows up in the unconditional obedience observed in nature:

> In nature, everything is unconditional obedience. The sighing of the wind, the echoing of the forest, the murmuring of the brook, the humming of the summer, the whispering of the leaves, the rustling of the grass, every sound, every sound you hear is all compliance, unconditional obedience. Thus you can hear God in it just as you hear him in the harmony that is the movement of the celestial bodies in obedience. The vehemence of the rushing winds, the buoyant flexibility of the clouds, the

---

7   Joy Division, "Love will Tear Us Apart," *Closer* (Factory Records, 1990).

droplet fluidity of the sea and its cohesion, the speed of light and the even greater of sound—it is all obedience. The rising of the sun on the hour and its setting on the hour, the shifting of the wind in a flash, the ebb and flow of the tide at specific times, and the agreement among the seasons in their precise alternating—all, all, all of it is obedience. Yes, if there were a star in the sky that wanted to have its own will, or a speck of dust on earth—they are wiped out at the same moment and with equal ease. In nature everything is nothing, understood in this way: it is nothing but God's unconditional will; the moment it is not unconditionally God's will, it ceases to exist. (Kierkegaard 1997, pp. 25-26)

To this I simply say, *Amen.*

Amen to the awareness that Kierkegaard shows regarding the ways that nature is not a manifestation of radical individualism, but of an essential harmony. Amen to the notion of community present in his vision of such harmony. Amen to the appreciation of the cohesion that serves to facilitate beauty.

This passage in Kierkegaard's text follows on the footsteps of his announcement that there is an absolute either/or decision regarding whether one will follow God or the world. We might narrate that decision as one of either seeking success or pursuing faithfulness. Kierkegaard's turn to nature is in the attempt to illustrate what it looks like to live in absolute commitment to God. This is a fascinating move on Kierkegaard's part because the obedience described as characterizing the choice of God over the applause of the social world is attributed to things that are not typically understood as beings capable of such agency. Birds, flowers, clouds, wind, these are seemingly quite different from humans when it comes to choice. We might be tempted to say that humans choose what to be and yet nature just is what it is. But, this realization is part of Kierkegaard's basic point. Nature obeys to such an extent that its freedom is manifest precisely in the absolute hearkening to God's call and command. Nature simply *is* faithful.

Having learned silence from the lilies and the birds, Kierkegaard then says that we should now learn to *obey*. Obedience is rarely viewed as a virtue, but more often gets presented as a slavish failure to live into one's own autonomy.

For Sartre, a life of obedience is reflective of living in bad faith—a denial of one's freedom and responsibility. For Nietzsche, obedience is a failure of will and ultimately an erasure of the potential divinity that resides in our human, all too human, lives. For Kant, obedience reflects a fundamental immorality rooted in a heteronymous conception of the source of our moral dignity. For Mill, Locke, and Rawls, albeit in various ways, obedience is often a sign of a flawed democracy that has forgotten the importance of liberty as the ground of human social existence. For contemporary feminists, critical race theorists, and queer theorists, obedience as a virtue for human identity risks just reinforcing the traditional power structures that have served to marginalize particular bodies as those who are expected to obey the voices of the privileged and empowered.

Admittedly, I tend to balk at the idea of obedience as a grounding virtue and so I find it much more complicated in Kierkegaard's trilogy of lessons to learn from the lilies and the birds than the initial silence and then ultimately joy. Maybe we can think with Kierkegaard a bit here and rethink how obedience can function as not merely a limit to agency, but potentially as a reflection of well-chosen directionality in one's life. In other words, we *should* want to follow the direction of, and receive the encouragement from, those who model virtue.

We have talked a lot about the way that faithfulness is not necessarily a confessional affirmation of the truth of theism, but instead an existential investment in a reflective commitment regarding where we draw our deepest inspiration, anchor our ultimate values, and motivate the activities that we deem worthy of our finitude. Yet, this means that we can't finally move in two directions at the same time. The simple Aristotelian point of logic—that X and non-X can't both be true at the same time and in the same respect—is ultimately one with serious existential import. This is a realization that echoes the thought of St. Augustine. Namely, the direction of our desire shapes the contours of our identity. Joy Division rightly acknowledges that the direction of our love will tear us apart if that direction is not shared with our beloved.

To love one thing is to reject something else as the ultimate object of that love. This can easily be seen when it comes to how we spend our time. What we do reflects what we value, and ultimately what we love. Yes, there are plenty of social and institutional obstacles to our time being radically responsive to our genuine agency. Poverty, historical injustice, marginalization, etc., all serve to strip away the freedom of finitude for far too many who have not benefited from the privilege of social identities that have been historically empowered. Nonetheless, we must own up to the fact that all of us make choices, so far as functionally possible given our social location, and far too often we choose to elevate the insignificant to the level of the ultimate. Doing so necessarily means degrading the ultimate to something short of its true value.

Like Open Mike Eagle, I need to offer an important *qualifier* here, though. I am not trying to answer the question for you regarding what is worthy of *your* ultimate value. Confronting that question for yourself is crucial to the task of selfhood. My goal is not to get you to agree with me in deciding what matters most, but to get you to take seriously the contingency, fragility, and yet urgency of that decision.

As Dietrich Bonhoeffer proposes, contra Martin Luther, we can always do otherwise! What we currently find ourselves loving is not obviously the only lovable thing. And, if we would spend the time and energy to be reflective and intentional, we might come to believe that it is not even worth loving in the first place. Precious little is obvious, and so we should take seriously our lived practices as revelatory. What we do, how we spend our time, who we choose to be with, these all reflect free decisions about love. But then decision itself is always reflective of who we are becoming as anchored in what we love.

I am now literally sitting on top of a mountain as I write these words. And at the risk of continued self-indulgence, let me give you a personal example to illustrate these Kierkegaardian lessons. This example actually brings me no small amount of shame, but it also now motivates me to do things differently—like finding ways to come to the mountains to write.

Here is my confession.

For many years, I spent more hours than I care to count, probably 80-100 of them a week, at the office—though I should note that my "office" was often random coffee shops and various tables in university libraries. I was trying to get a tenure track job, and then to get tenure, then trying to be promoted to Full Professor, etc. More important, though, than the external achievements being sought was the sense that I had to give everything that I had, and maybe everything I was, in order to be the best philosopher I could be. As I would often say: "I don't simply *teach* philosophy, I *am* a philosopher." And there's a difference. One can teach religion without being religious, or politics without being a politician. Similarly, one can hold a Ph.D. in philosophy without actually living into philosophy as a way of life. That said, I worked hard and as a result I accomplished a lot professionally. However, in those early days, it came at the cost of rarely seeing my wife. Sadly, there were many months where we would only see each other one day a week, despite living in the same house, because she was gone before I woke up and I didn't get home until after she was in bed.

Even though I got into academics in order to go fishing, I very rarely got to the rivers. There was just too much work to do. But *one day, eventually, then* I will fish a lot . . . or so I told myself.

I thought I could overcome the heavy stress by just working harder and pushing through to meet deadlines, and the more work I got done the better I perceived myself to be—not only at my job, but in my identity. Like Camus's comment about Sisyphus, I imagined myself happy because I was living into the dream that had motivated me throughout the pressures and exhaustion of graduate school. In many ways, the fact that I was able to do professional philosophy was a huge honor that humbled me on a regular basis. Indeed, I was now friends with the folks I had only previously read. I was now the president of the societies that just a few years earlier awed and intimidated me. I was editing the books and writing the articles that would help shape the field I cared so much about.

Look, I think all of this is important stuff, but then one day my wife and son and I were driving by my university with my parents, who were visiting from out of town, and my son, who was probably about 3 or 4 at the time, said "Grandma, look, that is Furman. That is where dad lives."

I was wrecked.
He was right.

That was where I *lived*. I had made my career more important than my family even though the entire time I told myself that I was putting in the hours in order to provide a better future *for my family*. But in believing this narrative and then making choices about my time that served to enact its truth, I was confusing the non-ultimate decision of time management with the ultimate decision of directional love. In other words, because I couldn't do everything, I was trying to do one thing really, really well. Unfortunately, the "one thing" ended up not being caring about my identity as a husband

and father, but caring about my identity as an academic. This doesn't mean that I didn't love my family, but simply that I was willing to love them less than something else, while telling myself I was doing the opposite.

Such is the nature of self-deception. I was effectively "obeying" the call of the office more than the "call" of my son. In this respect, my "love" was tearing me apart even before I realized that I was directionally misguided.

As is often the case in our lives, even when we "know" something, we often lack the courage, the will, or the integrity to reflect that knowledge in our practices. For one thing, being honest with ourselves in such ways can be hard work. So, as much as I wish that I could report that after that fateful day in the truck passing Furman I did things differently, I simply did not. I just felt guilty while continuing with the same old stuff. Although habits take some time to develop, they usually take even more time to break.

A couple years later, I was walking down the street in the city where I live and I had my son's hand in mine. He was probably 6 or 7 by this point, and out of the blue he said, "Dad, I don't want to be a philosopher when I grow up." To which I responded, with exaggerated bodily expressions, "What? Philosophers are the coolest!!!!" He then simply said, "No, dad, philosophers don't spend enough time with their kids."

Let that sink in. It did for me, instantly.
Ouch.

I had written dozens of essays about living meaningfully, finding truth, and seeking purpose, and yet in the words of a kid too young to appreciate irony, I was shown what I most loved and who it was making me. I probably don't have to tell you that I did not like what I saw. I was not ok with who I was becoming.

71

You would think that I would clearly have transformed my behavior, my time commitments, and my priorities after that, right? If you did, you would be wrong. It was not until the COVID pandemic (several more years later) that I finally started to change things. I wish I could say that I made such changes because I wisely willed the good and lived into it.

When I got promoted to Full Professor in the Spring of 2020, I came face to face with the fact that the green pasture I had been working so hard to enter was just one more field dotted with both weeds and flowers. Ultimately, it took a global pandemic shutting down my ability to choose to be away from my family to make me change. Sadly, external circumstances were required to facilitate an internal shift.

I can genuinely say that if it were not for COVID and the solitude and suffering that it brought with it, I would not be writing this book. I would still be burning the candle at both ends while telling my wife that *if* I can just get to finals, or get this next article done, or just finish another project, or just receive another grant, etc. etc. etc., that *then* I would be able to spend more time with her and with our son Atticus, fishing, hiking, and camping.

When the world shut down, it broke my habits. It freed me to escape the embodied routines of improper love that had, in effect, become invisible to me in my daily practice. In other words, the more that I worked the more it seemed like working was the only thing worth doing. But when I could no longer work in the same way, I had to figure out other ways of doing things. Thankfully, it also shifted what I *wanted* to do. That is, with the shift in habit came a shift in my enacted desire. *Now I would commit to doing all the things that originally motivated me to do all the things I was doing at the cost of not doing the things that I claimed to want to do.* Sheesh, that is a heck of a sentence, expressing an all-too-common heck of an existential plight. When I was unable to go to the office, I went to the mountains. That changed everything.

If only, then I'll . . .

This is a deadly logic.

The singer/songwriter Donovan Woods puts it really well when he says that so often we navigate our lives by saying "I'll do it next year."[8] This allows me to just get "this" done so that I can finally do "that." Simply put, "If only, then I'll . . ." is the grammar and the voice of delusion.

But, as Woods so poetically and profoundly notes, "there ain't no next year." Unless we are focused on living now toward what warrants our ultimate love, then next year will just be a Groundhog Day (or Nietzschean "eternal return of the same") where this year gets repeated over and over and over. One way or another, we are who we are becoming, and we become what we do.

To be honest, I am sure that some of my singular orientation was motivated by a distorted reading of Kierkegaard earlier in my life. The young Kierkegaard famously broke off his engagement to Regine Olsen in order to focus entirely, with the full singularity of his passion, as he would put it, on his authorship. To his credit, he believed fully that he was called to this vocation by God. The problem, though, is that he mistakenly understood that calling to be so radically singular that any deviation, or distraction, was considered a failure of faith. As he puts it later in his work, there is a purity of heart that emerges in "willing one thing" (Kierkegaard 1948). What might otherwise be a valuable and virtuous conception of earnestness in the direction of cultivated excellence, ended up leading to a failure to appreciate the flexibility required of finitude.

Because we don't have infinite time, we have to make good choices.

We obviously can't do everything. Alternatively, because of our

---

8   Donovan Woods, "Next Year," on *Both Ways* (Meant Well, 2018).

finitude, we will often face situations where we need to spend our time on what might appear to be a distraction in regard to one thing in order to focus intentionally on what matters more deeply. Although I admire Kierkegaard's singular focus, which would impress even the most devoted athlete or artist, it came at too high a cost for his happiness. And presumably this is true of Regine's happiness, at least if he had otherwise been able to get his act together. The same has been true in my own life.

I still love being a philosopher, but I care much more about living meaningfully in relationship with my son and wife than I do about leaving them with books I have written about cultivating meaningful relationships.

Unsurprisingly, such a commitment turns out not to detract from my philosophical work, but instead serves deeply to enrich it. I was not playing a zero-sum game after all. Yes, I still have to go the office, but I don't have to stay as long. Yes, I still have to write, and I genuinely love it, but I can strive to write about what is reflected in my lived practice. Indeed, I sometimes have to prioritize the concerns of my students or colleagues over the wants of my family, but I do not have to do so in absolute ways.

I still don't get to the mountains with Atticus as frequently as I would like to, due to the realities of his own school requirements as he is now finishing 7th grade, my own professional schedule, or the almost inevitable limitations of financial resources. Yet, living the life that we desire often takes far less money than we think (because it was never really, ultimately, about money, but about prioritizing our time). Ironically, our belief that we just need more money to do what we want serves to maintain the "if only, then I'll" logic. Our belief that it is an external constraint, rather than a failure of our own directional risk, that holds us back actually excuses our failures to own up to what our choices say about our loves. As Aaron James rightly notes, particular modes of capitalism often foster the increased prominence of assholes who dictate our time investments and narrate what we then consider "normal."

I don't literally have to go camping in order to choose to make my daily life reflective of the joys that going to the mountains facilitates. Watching our favorite YouTube videos before Atticus goes to bed, sitting in the backyard watching fireflies with Vanessa after he is asleep, remembering that drinking hot tea is always a good idea—this is all relational potential that can be fully embraced here and now. It is a choice to give into the loves that otherwise tempt us toward the "if only, then I'll" *logic of scarcity*.

We can alternatively choose to spend our time moving toward the expression and enjoyment of those loves that manifest a *logic of plentitude*. We may not be able to do everything, but we can do *this* . . . here, now.

We may not be able to live forever, but we can live on purpose. We may not be able to go everywhere, but we can surely strive, again with Anne Lamott, better to be where our feet are.

Decision is hard because it always amounts to a reflection of limitation. For example, we should care about excellence, but excellence at one thing means that we will necessarily be less excellent at something else. Even if we're excellent at juggling, we can't juggle everything excellently. The trick is to work at our decisions, our real choices, so that we are reflectively choosing the right aims—that is, the things that we fully and intentionally affirm as being worthy of our love. But, to imply that we can *only* will one thing, as Kierkegaard suggests, is simply false, unless that "one thing" were to be faithfully living into all our great ultimate values and loves, harmoniously.

We can, and must, will a bunch of things, but all those things should be consistent with the one ultimate love that guides our decision, grounds our value, and motivates our action. Sometimes you have to stay at the office late in order to finish the task, but sometimes you have to leave early to go get your son from school and hit the drive-thru for a milkshake. Yet, it is because we can and must do both that neither ends up overrunning their proper location in relation to our finitude. If I only ever stay at the office in order to write a marginally better article, then eventually I will find out that my lawn hasn't been mowed, my trash hasn't been taken to the curb, the garden hasn't been planted, and that my relationships are, like my house, beginning to grow weeds and show other signs of wear and lack of upkeep.

A few years ago I was trying to write a book on which I was woefully behind. In order to try to give me space to focus and get the work done, Vanessa took Atticus and went to Florida to visit her parents for a few weeks. I immediately sat down to write the next chapter and . . . *nothing*.

Absolutely nothing happened. Not a word.
I couldn't even get myself to the point where I cared at all about the book I had to write.

One afternoon, while sitting in front of a blank screen, I realized that a particular spot in our yard would be a great place for a patio and fire-pit. I closed my computer, grabbed my gloves, and went to the landscape supply store. For the next two weeks, all I did was work on the patio. It turned out great, or at least as great as I could make it, given my lack of expertise in patio building. As soon as I finished it, I opened my computer, and to my surprise, the writing came easily. Because I had allowed my brain, my body, and my spirit to refocus for a while, I was able to find the energy and direction I had been lacking.

Let me be clear here, I do not mean to suggest that just by doing yard work we will somehow get inspired to write philosophy. It may have worked for Epicurus in his garden, but such efforts aren't usually needed for most of us. All I am saying is that my building the patio was not ultimately at odds with my writing my book and loving my family. They were all part of each other and came together toward my aims of faithfully being a husband, a father, and a philosopher. These are not conflicting values or ultimately opposed directions. Nonetheless, they can seem to be in conflict anytime that we think that what matters most is *the* patio, or *the* book, etc.

If I *only* work hard on one thing like a book, and see it as the ultimate manifestation of my identity, then I will lose my family. If I *only* spend time with my family, and refuse to situate my relationships within the context of social structures, I will eventually lose the house in which we live. If I *only* build the patio, and see it as the exclusive evidence of my excellence, I will get fired, or lose a publishing contract, or fade into professional oblivion. If I *only* write books, and see them as the singular example of good thinking, I will not have a patio on which to sit with those I love while thinking about the next book worth writing.

In ultimate things, the decision is absolute. But, in relation to that absolute decision, lots of non-ultimate things will need to become important as temporal priorities at specific times. The tricky part is keeping the ultimate in focus, despite the flexible finite engagements. When I write my book, am I still doing so out of love for my son? When I love my son, am I still caring about my work and my students? When I mow the lawn, am I still thinking about my next book? When I think about my next book, am I continuing to pull the weeds from the lawn? And the list continues.

It might seem like I have just made things worse, because now we can't ever rest easy in our decisions, but always have to remain vigilant that they are genuinely reflective of the many loves we continue to embrace as potentially conflicting ultimates. This is certainly a risk against which we should guard.

With this general point in mind, Emmanuel Levinas (1987, pp. 155-156) says that "insomnia" is the best descriptor of what it is like to take the task of a moral life seriously. Levinas realizes that it would be easier not to have to own up to the conflicting responsibilities that animate our moral existence. However, those responsibilities don't vanish just because we turn away from them. The decision about what is ultimately worthy of love does not get avoided just because we give in to society's trivial priorities. In the end, risk remains. But that is what makes decisions matter. We do not have to understand ourselves as living internal to a Sisyphean tragedy—he was condemned to roll a rock up a hill and immediately upon arriving at the top the rock would roll back down . . . for all eternity! Instead, we can rethink this story and now "imagine Sisyphus (and ourselves) happy" because we have our rock to roll. As long as Sisyphus has his rock, he has purpose, he has momentum. Like him, we have our love to enact and pursue. Again, the goal is not successfully to stop pushing the rock once and for all, but to continue to push it ever more faithfully each day.

With this framework in place, we can better understand that obedience is not a matter of abdicating our agency, but of undertaking the hard work that love requires.

Kierkegaard's account of the "either/or" faced by the lilies and the birds is helpful so long as we remember that it is about ultimately choosing God *or* the cheers of the crowd, the influence of popularity, and the security that privilege affords. That is, faithful investment in what matters or a devotion to external success that eventually prevents us, slowly but surely, from being able to see what matters as anything other than what others praise us for doing. We might be still living lives of obedience, but in that case just, only obeying "them." Following "their" instruction on how to live in relation to what "they" think can seem so important.

But there is another option.

Nature is uninterested in what "they" say. The lilies and the birds don't care about likes on Facebook, or the smiles and frowns of colleagues. The trees and clouds are not showing off for Instagram (#nofilter). The wind and waters are not motivated by how many shares they inspire on TikTok. They all do what they do because it is who they are as properly related to God—that is, to the ultimate object of their being and their love. What we love determines who we are becoming and so who we will be. In obedience, the lilies and the birds are becoming who they are meant to be as lilies and birds.

Who are you becoming?
Who or What is your God?

These questions are just different versions of our original question "What is worthy of your finitude?" In the difficult hours of everyday life, there are no polytheists. We are all, each and every one of us, theists about something and atheists about almost everything else. Saying yes to one God means saying no to all the possible others. This is a simple point about language, logic, and the metaphysics of truth claims.

The same is true for obedience. What or who will you obey? Bob Dylan presses us with this question when he says that we all "gotta serve somebody."[9] Having learned silence, we must learn obedience. But, when we learn obedience, we are now capable of learning joy.

Silence not only makes listening possible, but also it cultivates hospitality to the voices of others.

Obedience not only reveals the object of our love, but also it helps us to orient our lives in relation to that love.

Joy not only stands at the conclusion of our decision, but also animates the significance of our decision in the first place.

---

9   Bob Dylan, "Gotta Serve Somebody," on *Slow Train Coming* (Columbia, 1979).

Joy Division is right that love will break your heart, but Kierkegaard's point is that the joy *Decision* modeled by the lilies and the birds helps our hearts to keep beating in rhythm with the glorious harmony that is the narrative of our lives in obedience to a God worthy of worship.

6

JUST SEND IT!
LEARNING ETHICS ON THE TRAIL

When I am hiking, backpacking, or mountain biking, I am rarely thinking about the finer contours of moral theory. This is unlikely to come as a great surprise to anyone, except maybe for the former student of mine who was on the football team and always wanted to talk about philosophy on the sidelines during the games. I eventually had to tell the eager student that I was there to watch football, not to discuss phenomenological hermeneutics. He seemed a bit disappointed in me. But there are times to "sideline" even such a vital activity as philosophy. When I am on the trail hiking, or dropping in a downhill run on my bike, or setting up camp, I am fully invested in the activity at hand. Indeed, if I am actively reflective about philosophical topics in the midst of such behavior, it increases the likelihood that I will forget something, or make a mistake in ways that I will quickly regret.

Part of getting good at being in the mountains, or in any other activity where progress is possible, is finding a way to be simultaneously fully aware and deeply relaxed. Aaron James (2012) refers to this as "finding the flow" and suggests that it requires the skill of "adaptive attunement." What he means by this idea is that we have to be flexible enough to move well in relation to what we are given. When the trail leads to a sharp turn followed by a 5ft drop, appropriate bodily movement in specific directions is absolutely necessary: weighting your outside foot, turning your knees in the direction of the turn, moving rearward in order to unweight the front of the bike on the drop, etc. are all crucial. Attempting to force things to your will on the trail is rarely going to turn out well.

Rocks are harder than bones. Trees are bigger than bodies. Bears are faster than you.

Learning to adapt, to move with what the terrain is doing, is crucial. The only way to adapt in responsible ways is to be fully attuned to what is going on. As Rage Against the Machine and Lamb of God both again scream at us all, "wake up!"[10]

Pay attention. Be fully present.

If you are not attuned, you will not be able to adapt.
If you refuse to adapt, your attunement is worthless.

I was once backpacking with a friend of mine from graduate school. We had been hiking about 10 miles or so and he was walking in front of me. Well, as anyone who has ever followed someone else in a car will know, it is easy to focus on the car in front of you and get in a wreck because you are no longer watching everything else going on in traffic. That is basically what happened to me. I was hiking along, he and I were talking, and I was unconsciously following him while just ignoring everything else. Then, *bam*! I hit something with my head and immediately went down like a sack of potatoes. It turns out that since he is significantly shorter than I am, he went under a large tree branch without ducking and I went . . . *directly*

---

10   Rage Against the Machine, "Wake Up," on *Rage Against the Machine* (Epic Records, 1992); Lamb of God, "Memento Mori," *Lamb of God* (Epic, 2020).

into it with my forehead. Ouch. Because I was not attuned to my context, I was unable to adapt appropriately to it.

Having recovered from that impact, let me be clear that a part of living faithfully, philosophically, and purposively is knowing *when* to be reflective and *when* to be actively engaged. When you are on the trail, I encourage the latter in order to avoid walking into a tree branch that will prevent you from doing the former effectively once you make camp and are sitting around the fire.

Even if I rarely think about the moral life while hiking or riding trails, that doesn't mean I am not still enacting an awareness of moral expectations. Being on the trail introduces a whole host of such considerations about how one "should" act in relation to other people using the trail and the natural world around us.

Although these moral expectations must initially be taught—for example, when I am riding with my son, I am helping him to learn things such as those going uphill have the right of way, stay on the trail when riding single-track, don't skid when the trails are muddy in order to protect the trail itself, etc.—the rules only really become alive in us when they become part of our ordinary behavior.

In this way, morality works like mountain biking. Comfortably navigating the sharp turn and subsequent drop requires that we do not simply know what to do as a conceptual idea, but actively know what to do, and how to do it, in our *bones*. It has become habit. It comes naturally. Our body just does it without our having to think about it as an intentional commitment. For all the neuroscientists in the room, we might say that our brains need to work faster than our minds, like a major league batter instinctively swinging at a fastball he'd never have time to ponder in order to plan his move. That is why biking requires practice. Morality also requires practice. It has to be embodied as a habit that gives rise to doing the "right thing" as a normal fact of our lived action.

When I teach my son the moral expectations of being on the trail, I don't do this so that he can pass a test on moral theory when we get back to the truck (#worstcampingtripever). Instead, I do it so that it will become part of who he is and how he conducts himself *without* thinking. Virtue is not ultimately about following rules set by someone else, but about internalizing those ideas that lead to human flourishing in ways that make them what we unconsciously expect of ourselves.

Upon reflection, I think that the ethics we learn and then embody on the trail is a great place to look for general guidelines about how to live more broadly wherever we find ourselves. There are lots of ways we could summarize things, here, but for the sake of clarity and concision, I want to propose that there really three key aspects to these moral expectations: *humility, hospitality*, and *gratitude*.

Humility
We have already thought a lot about humility as an epistemic requirement for responsible life, but in our consumer driven selfie-culture it is a point worth repeating over and over. Unless we are humble, we are unwilling to make revisions and adjust or adapt to things as they come. Pride that displaces humility might plausibly be viewed as the source of all vice because it speaks to the fact that we think we are sufficient unto ourselves and, thus, don't need anything or anyone else. Moral life, at its core, is a matter of attempting to do/get/be better than we are currently. It is premised on humility. If you want to be good, then you must be humble enough to admit that you still have work to do.

I have been a drummer for many years. I was a session player for a while and toured widely with various groups. Accordingly, I have spent a lot of time around professional musicians. The very best of them, like the very best athletes, and the very best craftspeople, and so on, are those who are the first to recognize that they are not yet perfect. Excellence, like ethics, is about continued faithfulness, not finished success.

The same is true on the trail. The best backpackers, the best rock climbers, and the best mountain bikers all share with top musicians the commitment to the importance of the tireless necessity of continued practice. They don't practice in order to get good enough to stop practicing. They practice so that their practice becomes ever more advanced, to the point that what was formerly very hard is now quite easy. And yet they keep an eye on what remains difficult. Practice isn't about overcoming difficulty, but rather about raising the level regarding where it is located.

Prideful people don't practice. Why would they? Why should they?

Humble people sometimes don't practice enough, but they acknowledge that fact and then try to keep practicing.

Being on the trails fosters an ethic of humility because we are constantly reminded of our smallness, of our fragility, and of our limitations. And yet, as Socrates constantly reminds us, humility is not at odds with confidence. It is the condition for *appropriate* confidence. We might say that the goal is not to be the best in the room, but rather to be in the room with the best.

One of the most dangerous things while biking is hitting a feature, like a jump, drop, rock garden, or whatever, with hesitancy. Bikers encourage each other not to be hesitant by saying, "Just send it!" This doesn't mean to be stupid or pay no attention to the danger. Quite the opposite. Usually, this phrase gets said only after spending time walking the feature, looking at it from different angles, then doing a few "run ups" where you ride up to the challenge as if you are going to do it, but then stop just before it in order to make sure you are taking the right "line" and anticipating all the different ways through. It's like a golfer scoping out the lay of the green before making her putt. In the course of all this practice, the humbly confident biker is attuned to what the feature presents, and then adapts in order best to ride it.

"Just send it!" is not offered as a disregard for risk, but as a recognition of the confidence needed to navigate any risk with responsible awareness—with the right degree of adaptive attunement.

Humility, thus, should not be confused with hesitancy.

Hesitancy is dangerous on trails because it causes your foot to slip where it needs to hold fast, it makes you cower when you need to "get big" (like when faced with a bear), and it inclines you to pull up when you need to push forward. Confidence actually requires an inner humility insofar as confidence is not a matter of thinking you are perfect, but of realizing that when you bow to the circumstances, when you notice, watch, and submit to the contours of the reality you confront, you are capable of navigating the challenge while still admitting that there are no guarantees that it will go well. As Derrida, Kierkegaard, Bonhoeffer, Beauvoir, and pretty much all existentially oriented thinkers remind us, there is no faith without risk.

But what does any of this have to do with ethics? It seems like humility can be an important *epistemic* virtue as pertains to selfhood, but how does this *morally* implicate us?

Humility is necessarily situated in the context of a shared world. As signs all over the mountains read: "Share the trail." Being humble is not just a matter of admitting you don't do everything perfectly, as important as we have seen that awareness to be. It is also about recognizing that your aims, goals, and hopes always occur alongside those of others. Your desire to "session" or practice a feature over and over in order to do it better is important, but doing so without a concern for others might cause them to be unable to ride that feature because you are in the way.

This general awareness that the trail highlights nicely fits with the thought of the philosopher, Emmanuel Levinas. He suggests that "ethics is first philosophy." That might seem like a strange claim in all sorts of ways, but his point is that traditionally philosophy has started from a theory about what things *are* (ontology) and only afterwards turned to what they *should be* (ethics). In simple terms, philosophy has largely prioritized description over normativity. There are many advantages to this traditional approach. For one thing, unless we have a general sense of what something is, it is hard to know if we can even attribute a moral dimensions to it. Ethics, it might seem, is only possible for some beings, and so an ontological description of that difference at least appears to be logically prior to an ethical account of what "ought" to be the case for those beings. Or, as we Southerners might say, "You can't expect to get much work done if you stay in bed."

However, despite some commonsense reasons to think that ontology is foundational for philosophical inquiry, Levinas warns that this traditional approach can make it seem like ethical life is an optional add-on, or merely a supplemental possibility, rather than an intrinsic part of our identity. More particularly, that ontological approach makes it seem like who we "are" is somehow isolated, self-sufficient, and unentangled from any conception of who we ought to be, and what we ought to do, or become. On this model, ethics would only arise as a question after the fact of our existence, due to our contingent circumstances of being with others. In this way, Levinas provocatively states that ontology has traditionally been rooted in an implicit egoism. Our description of ourselves has classically been predominantly self-referential.

Levinas doesn't accept this traditional ontological account due to the way that our very experience in the world is one that makes such isolated self-sufficiency implausible. Our very existence in so many ways, he realizes, depends upon our relationship, and responsibility to, others. Our birth is a result of our parents' actions. Our development as a child is due to the care given to us by others. Our sense of the world is itself occasioned by a whole network of social, cultural, and educational contexts that have been established by others preceding us. So, rather than being a self who then takes up ethical responsibility, Levinas inverts this orientation. On his account, selfhood is always already a response to others for whom and to whom I am responsible in various ways.

Another French philosopher, Jean-Louis Chrétien (2004), who we will consider in more detail in the following chapters, expands this idea and contends that there is a basic structure that conditions subjective existence itself. He terms this structure the "Call/Response." The idea is that we exist as a response to a call from another that precedes us.

The "call" here is not meant to be literal. Instead, it is the name Chrétien gives to the idea that selfhood is never its own condition. In other words, selfhood is never able to stand on its own, but depends on something else. Chrétien's account is sort of like when you are walking down the street and you hear "Hey, you!" To such a "call," the typical response is "Who, me?" Levinas and Chrétien both suggest that, in that moment, there in the recognition of the other who calls out to us, we find the first moment of our own selfhood. I do not exist (ontology) and only later encounter others (ethics). I emerge as the one who bears the responsibility to turn and reply. For the finite human, existence and ethics embrace from the start. Our identity is formed by the recognition that our subjectivity is conditioned by our relationships to others.

As Levinas will put it, sociality precedes individuality and responsibility precedes freedom.

Now, this might seem like an odd claim, given that we are so accustomed to thinking about ourselves in radically individual ways. Consider, though, that even the phrase championed by so many individualistic libertarians, "Don't tread on me!" is itself a necessary recognition of the relation to others. The "me" in the phrase doesn't exist separately, but rather occurs as a response to the fact that others are already there. In the same vein, Jean-Paul Sartre (1989) has a character in his play, *No Exit*, provocatively claim that "hell is other people" precisely because Sartre sees that the fact of essential responsibility wrecks our ability to think that we are essentially independent beings.

The task is not to make the most of oneself, but to make the most of what has been made of you.

Let's get back on the trails.

Think about it . . . the trail you did not build but are now riding or hiking stands, in some respect, as the call of the other, perhaps many others, and our hiking and riding it serves as a response to their investment in a shared world. How we approach the trail speaks to our relation to those others who built the trail, and all who have enjoyed it before us, but also to those others who will ride or hike it after us.

One of the greatest complements I have ever received was when someone told me that every house in which I had lived was better when I left than when I arrived. The landscaping, the repairs, the beautification, etc., all spoke to my investment in making where I was as good as possible, not only because others would eventually inherit that work I had done, but also because it matters that we intrinsically care about our spaces. When we move our bike aside to allow the people going uphill to have the right of way, when we carry out all of our trash from camp, when we release the fish that we catch, when we stay on the marked trail rather than destroying the wildlife around it, we live into the humility that ethics as first philosophy requires.

Being on the trails constantly reminds us that it is not all about you or me.

Inviting others to "ride with us," both metaphorically and literally, helps us to overcome the persistent temptations of egoism that so pervasively characterize our culture. Being confident about our beliefs and actions is much more comfortably displayed when we do not see ourselves as in conflict with everyone else, but when we see the community in which we find ourselves as the very condition of the individual joys toward which we, like the birds and lilies, *ultimately*, strive.

In faithfulness, and with humility, we ride or hike (and live) together.

Hospitality

Humility on its own, however, is insufficient as a moral virtue. It must be accompanied by, and then open onto, the practice of hospitality. The reason for this transition should be pretty clear. If we acknowledge our limitations, our implicit bias, and our egoism, then we should strive to overcome such things so far as possible. But that means being receptive to, and welcoming of, the voices, views, and expertise of others who may instruct, correct, or augment our own perspectives.

Here we can return to René Descartes trademark argument for the existence of God that we considered earlier. I think that his argument actually parallels trail ethics regarding hospitality.

Descartes's claim is that our awareness of our imperfections, coupled with any knowledge of what perfectibility would involve, requires that there be a perfect being. Getting into the specifics of the argument would take us too far afield here, but a reminder about the basic contours is perhaps helpful. The essential idea is that if we were the only existent beings, then we would never be able to be aware of things better than ourselves. However, because we do have ideas of perfection that outstrip our own abilities, there must be some being who instantiates those perfections in ways that then get imprinted in us as the source of the ideas. Descartes's argument faces all sorts of philosophical problems in its effort to demonstrate the existence of a God, but along the way he hits at something pretty important: *humility requires that we be willing to learn, and learning requires hospitality to being instructed by others.*

This should be pretty obvious. When we feel like we could do things better, we must have some sense that things could be otherwise than they are now. This awareness of a basic, but inescapable, contingency, the reality of our current state of development are as merely one among many available alternatives, is what facilitates humility as a possibility. But mere acknowledgement of contingency, which is the idea that things could have been different, would not, on its own, make humility a moral virtue. Instead, humility names contingency as the condition of progress. That is a really technical philosophical way of making a pretty simple point: we should realize that things could be different if we ever hope to make them change. As the rapper Busdriver proclaims, "we can make it better."[11]

Ok, sure, but *how*, though? Only by admitting that we can't lean on our own understanding alone. We need to be confident enough to look beyond ourselves for answers. Enter the virtue of hospitality.

Humility knows that critique is possible, but hospitality is the lived practice of being open to others, seeking them out, and then receiving the potential critique that they may offer to us in order that we might improve ourselves, and our shared situation.

Not only that, though. Hospitality is also a matter of our opening spaces for others to flourish.

Let me try to give you an example of how humility and hospitality come together as such an invitation.

On days when I can't get to the mountains, I often ride my hardtail bike on a paved trail in the city where I live. Doing this allows me to build up endurance and improve my fitness. The trail used to be a railway track but was converted as a community improvement project. It's extremely popular and is frequently full of families with kids riding together. Although there are signs that say "stay to the right, pass on the left with care," I can report from experience that it is

---

11   Busdriver, "Ego Death," featuring Aesop Rock and Danny Brown, on *Perfect Hair* (Big Dada, 2014).

tough to get your kids to stay where they need to be. Moreover, things like checking over their shoulders before moving around people is hard when they are first learning to ride. Accordingly, if you plan to ride on the trail on the weekend, then you need to expect that it is going to be difficult to ride with any sustained speed. Nonetheless, that doesn't prevent more advanced riders from acting like they are training for the Tour de France. And, although there are plenty of exceptions, it is often those "pros-in-their-own-mind" who get most frustrated with everyone else who they perceive as "in their way."

While riding recently, I was in front of my son who was riding with a friend beside him. Naturally, my son and his friend tended to take up more of the trail than they should have because they wanted to talk to each other. I did keep telling them why that was dangerous and teaching them the right ways to approach folks was to fall in behind each other so there was plenty of room for others to pass. In fact, "on your left" is now a common phrase my son says when just out in the world walking by other people!

However, at one point, some dude came tearing down the trail and instead of slowing down a bit, he just yelled for my son to "get your head up!" My son braked and tried to pull in behind his friend, but clearly not quickly enough for the world's next Lance Armstrong. Full of bro-energy, the guy narrowly avoided hitting him and then yelled again in frustration as he passed.

Yes, my son should have been paying more attention. Yes, my son knew better than to be alongside someone on a narrow two-way trail. But the amped up dude also failed to show appropriate hospitality to others sharing the trail with him. That guy's behavior did not display the spirit of a shared activity, or in any way make my son want to keep riding. Instead, as we have learned from Aaron James, he was being an asshole who viewed everyone else as in *his* way.

Those who display hospitable excellence encourage others to keep going even if it means that they need to slow down. Those who are arrogantly mediocre think that others need to clear the road as they pass because they are the only people that matter.

This is the way that the success-orientation of our world so often works. Assholes tend to think that the world is made for them. In this approach to life, they not only refuse to realize their own frailties, but also they fail to open spaces for other people to become great at the thing that they present themselves as having mastered.

Hospitable people want others to get better so that the community can progress beyond where it is.

Inhospitable people are threatened by the excellence of others and so try to prevent others from growing.

Hospitable people move aside to allow others to pass.

Inhospitable people make sure that they get to set the pace and force everyone else to adjust.

I admit that when I am out hiking or biking and come up behind a big crowd of folks, a church group or scout troop or something, I am tempted by frustration. But I am almost always surprised that they quickly move aside to let me pass without perceiving it as a problem for them. And, usually, they encourage me as I move through, with positive wishes like: "Have a good hike!" or "Enjoy your ride." It is such a small thing, but it can be world changing.

Perhaps our political leaders should spend more time hiking, or at least find more opportunities to bike to work. Maybe then they would appreciate that genuine leadership is not about being better than others, but about findings ways to invite others to become as good as possible.

Nationalism, we might say, is the absolute enemy to all genuine patriotism. Showing hospitality and sharing the trail is an important microcosm of what it means to share the world. Libertarianism as a political theory is flawed if it assumes that caring about oneself allows for, or even requires, disregarding others. Libertarianism on the trail is vicious if it leads to behavior that does not make others want to get back on the trail more often.

The ethics of the trail teaches us that making room for others actively facilitates more room for yourself. If that dude who almost hit my son on the path had shown hospitality, he would have understood that slowing down a bit and making sure that my son saw him with plenty of time to move over would likely have been a better way to teach a 13-year-old to pay more attention to what was ahead of him, or around him. Instead, he just made my son scared, me angry, and proved that he was an asshole. Maybe he was just practicing to run for Congress.

Gratitude
Anne Lamott (2012) says that her three favorite prayers are "Help. Thanks. Wow." These are great prayers. We have already thought some about two of them in various ways. "Help" illustrates the importance of humility and hospitality, and "Wow" highlights the joy we should learn from the lilies and the birds. We haven't yet talked much about "Thanks," but we should.

Why is showing gratitude so difficult on so many occasions? I think it is intimately intertwined with humility and hospitality. Saying "thanks" requires us to be humble enough to admit that we needed help. Asking for help, in turn, means that we have to be hospitable enough to receive assistance from others.

Without humility there is no need for gratitude.
Without hospitality, there is no occasion for gratitude to be practiced.

Our world is not one in which gratitude is commonly viewed as either an individual virtue or a social good. The reasons that we could give for this are likely to vary depending on whether one is an historian, a sociologist, or as in my case, a philosopher. Martin Luther King Jr. once said that "justice is what love looks like in public." Well, gratitude is what a life defined by humility and hospitality looks like in public. Gratitude, like justice, is in direct contrast to the capitalistic success-logic that says the more you have the better you are. It is an awareness of what has been provided for you, given to you, and made possible for you. Returning to Levinas and Chrétien, we might say that being grateful illuminates the fact that self-sufficiency (as an ontological and moral conception—again remember the distinction between existential aloneness and ethical aloneness) is not only a problematic, and egoist, ideal, but it is also a practical impossibility.

Gratitude names that we are not only beings-with-others, but that we are beings who exist *because of* others.

That said, showing gratitude doesn't necessarily need a discrete object to whom it is directed. As Martin Buber might say, gratitude neither requires an I-Thou relation (person to person), nor an I-It relation (person to thing). Gratitude can be more of a Thoreauian way of life—an implicit mode of inhabiting the world rather than an explicit attitude or expression directed in particular to someone or something. It is this sense of gratitude as a more pervasive mindset that I think we can discover "on the trail" when we focus on faithfulness rather than success.

For those who are success minded, the goal of hiking, fishing, biking, camping, or whatever else one does in the mountains is largely tied to a specific quantifiable outcome. A record time on the downhill run, a trophy brook trout, a long-distance thru-hike, etc. are all cool things and well worth striving for. However, as we have seen in numerous ways, if those goals are "ultimate," then we are not invested, *ultimately*, in living. For those directed toward faithfulness, however, the ultimate goal is ever to be becoming the person who goes to the mountains, takes adventures in the woods, and spends time in the river or stream. It is about prioritizing those activities, that time, those experiences, and those values as central to one's selfhood . . . not as an accomplishment, but as a *way of life*.

As I will explain in Chapter Eight, I do not go fishing in order to catch the trophy fish, though that is surely something I do desire to some degree, but instead to be someone who enacts fishing as worthy of my finitude. I do not bike in order to set records on the downhill run, though I do try to get faster when I can, but instead I ride to be someone who finds that spending time on a mountain bike fosters a life without regret.

When we focus on faithfulness rather than success, we invite gratitude as a way of life because faithfulness is a matter of being thankful for the life that we are actively invested in living.

Probably not surprisingly, I watch a lot of YouTube videos about trout fishing, mountain biking, overlanding (exclusively in Toyota Tacomas I should note), and hiking. It is true that those videos talk a lot about strategies for success—as concerns having the right gear, cultivating the right knowledge, and engaging in the right practices. And yet, if you watch very long you will almost always notice the bikers, hikers, and fishers just pausing and standing in awe of what it is that they get to do, how it is that they spend their time, and what it is that constitutes the beauty of the spaces that they inhabit.

I remember one video where a guy was riding a trail really hard and ended up crashing. Thankfully he was not injured. But, while he sat there on the ground with his bike laying off to the side, he just sighed and looked out at the mountains and said, "Wow, no matter how your day goes on the trail, this is ultimately why we ride." The "this" to which he was referring was nebulously directed at not only the sublime vista, but also at the full experience and feeling of being alive that the crash brought into full relief. He was not saying "thank you" to someone, but simply inhabiting gratitude for being able to be right there where he was.

Gratitude doesn't have to be cashed out as a grand metaphysical gesture. It can happen in the most mundane aspects of life.

For example, I was raised in the South and so learning my "please" and "thank yous" as a sign of respect was ingrained in me from a very early age. There are many, many things about being a Southerner, or a human, for that matter, that are deeply problematic in our time (widespread systemic racism, staggering class disparity, gendered assumptions that reinforce patriarchy, rampant homophobia, and much more), but this focus on respect is one particular aspect of the South that I love, along with iced tea with lots of lemon!

My Southern upbringing taught me to cultivate an awareness of my dependency on the actions of others as facilitating my flourishing. This allowed me to normalize gratitude, and thus largely make an invisible assumption of my proper embodiment of it. Such Southern "hospitality" as it is often called, often serves as just a mask for behind-the-scenes self-aggrandizement. This masking phenomenon can be seen easily in the infamous phrase: "Well, bless her heart." This locution is rarely deployed as a sincere concern for the wellbeing of another. Instead, it is often a way of presenting some measure of critique or disregard under a performative cloak of care or kindness.

And yet, what if we all, like the folks seeking faithfulness in the mountains, started living lives of hospitality—"please"—and gratitude—"thank you." Rather than just saying, "Bless her heart," we might then do the work that actually blesses others. We could move beyond "thoughts and prayers" to policies and actions. Said slightly differently, doing so might encourage us to supplement get-well cards with equitable healthcare.

Humility, hospitality, and gratitude are not merely matters of personal concern, they are also matters of social justice.

Such a shift in our perception and our practices would go a long way toward changing the tone of our social engagement and the priorities that we have allowed to define our public spaces. If we could learn from the great bikers, the hikers, and the fishers about how to live, we might see humility, hospitality, and gratitude as not merely instrumental goods that lead to winning friends and influencing enemies in the name of cultivating our brand and maximizing our profits. Rather, we might see these three virtues as simply the backbones of our *life together*, as Dietrich Bonhoeffer (1954) would contend.

So, regardless of whether you are religious or not, Southern or not, a fan of iced tea or not, let's all make a habit of living the prayers, "Help me. Thank you. Wow." And then, while being attuned and adapting to what comes, find ways every day, whether biking in the mountains on standing in line at Wal-Mart, to *send it!*

7

From a Sigh to a Self: Responding to Calls and Learning to Walk

John Muir famously claimed that "The mountains are calling and I must go." I think that Muir and I must have phone numbers that are quite close to each other since I get the same call quite often (like that *Seinfeld* episode where Kramer keeps getting calls for "Movie Phone"). In light of the proliferation of workshops, retreats, and organizations devoted to helping people "find their calling," I think it is worth bringing a bit of philosophical attention to the idea of calling.

Maybe in responding to the call of the mountains, we can learn to silence the notifications on our cell phones and lean in more closely to the wisdom of the lilies and the birds. It is important to do so as we think well about what is worthy of our finitude. If we don't pause and do such careful thinking, then what we take to be our calling might just end up being the empty affirmation of an echo chamber facilitated by social media, a success orientation, and the preferences of assholes. Deciding on the direction of our risk, on who it is that we hope to become, requires being invested in not only *finding* our calling, but also *responding* adequately/responsibly/ faithfully to it.

In order to think through these issues, in this chapter I am not going to focus on what happens once we get to the mountains, but instead I am going to pay attention to the music playing in the truck on the way there. Listen with me and let's see if we can begin to hear whatever it is that calls us a bit more clearly. The goal is to learn to distinguish between those calls that should impact us in the task of becoming a self, as opposed to those that should be ignored in order that we not lose ourselves in the general "sigh" of despair that defines what Kierkegaard terms the "leveling" that occurs in the herd mentality. Let's see if we can find ways to move from a "sigh" to a "self."

Speaking of the downward pressures toward mediocrity, let's talk about the rapper (if we can legitimately call him that), Drake.

I do not like Drake. I think his work is generally bad for the art form of hip hop. I am not entirely sure what bothers me so much about him—probably a combination of things—but I know that his 2016 hit "Hotline Bling" does not help his case. Let's listen to some of the "wisdom" that he presents therein:

> You used to call me on the cell phone,
> late night when you need my love.
> I know when that hotline bling,
> that can only mean one thing.[12]

Sigh.

I take seriously the idea presented by Leo Tolstoy (1912) that we should be actively aware of the "wisdom of children" that can sometimes be missed in our all too adult way of being—which often just means being serious and boring with a good dash of egoism thrown in. Within the logic of asshole culture and the success orientation, usually this paradigmatic "adultness" is characterized simply

---

12   Drake, "Hotline Bling," on *Views* (Cash Money Records, 2016).

as "acting like a professional." Professionalism, on this model, ends up being a euphemism for *selling out* in the name of *selling more*. Is there a way to do the hard work that excellence requires without "falling prey" (a notion developed by Heidegger in relation to the temptation of the "they") in ways that eschew faithfulness as a way of life?

I think that there is.
Perhaps I expect too much.

Kierkegaard's encouragement that the knight of faith finds the "sublime in the pedestrian" can invite us to reconsider Drake. Maybe he can tell us something if we are maximally charitable to his "childlike" wisdom—of course, if his songs are any indication, usually he is a child of about 16 who has just discovered how cool sex and money are.

Here is my thought: Drake actually does an excellent job of presenting a *reductio ad absurdum* regarding the idea of vocation, or a call. In other words, he shows us how we should *not* understand such notions.

We will come back to Drake in a bit, but first I want to think about what it means, philosophically, to respond to a call.

A call is always phenomenologically distinctive in three ways:

1. It calls *to someone*. Even if anonymous in its origin, it is never anonymous in its reception.
2. It always comes *from somewhere*; though it is an open question whether it must come from someone.
3. It calls *for something*. It is not declarative, but inquisitive.

We might understand these three characteristics as Ethico-religious, Ontological, and Epistemic, respectively.

The philosopher Jean-Louis Chrétien (2004), who we have already considered a bit in the previous chapter, writes a lot about the idea of a call and he argues that the call is never possible without a response. Indeed, he goes so far as suggesting that the call is only ever heard *in* the response itself. The existential phone rings, we might say, only when we decide either to pick it up or to ignore it. A jangling or buzzing phone without such a response is not a call, but merely a sound. It becomes a call when a response is given in one way or another.

I know that this sounds weird. How can we respond to something if it doesn't exist prior to our response? The call comes first, and only then can we respond, right!?

Well, think about it: calls are distinguished from questions precisely along this phenomenological line. When we ask a question, the answer is not what constitutes the question as a question. Indeed, merely the grammatical mark of a curly thing with a dot under it does that work, or at least in English, a question can be formulated simply with a certain tonal raising of one's voice. At least that is the way that it *seems*. With a bit more careful attention, though, we can begin to appreciate why calls are not obviously reducible to such "questions." Whereas questions do not require answers, but are capable of standing on their own, calls are different. A call *becomes* a call only when we respond, when we constitute them as calls by treating them as such.

Ok, I imagine that you are now thinking: "Yep, this is why philosophy is useless. . . Where is my cell phone?"

Though I grant that philosophy can often seem esoteric and detached from lived practice, let me encourage you, just for a few minutes, to suspend any general annoyance with the way philosophers think about things and, instead, realize that sometimes it is only when we look at things in ways that most other folks don't that we begin to see what we, and they, usually miss.

We will see whether my reflections in this book will turn out to have been a call to you—but if I am right, it will all depend on how *you choose to respond.*

The point is that a call occurs in its being *interpreted as* a call. Said a bit sexier, we could claim that a call is never without contextual framing. It is not hermeneutically transparent. Instead, it is always dependent on the decisions of the respondent. Importantly, not just anything can count as a response. For example, we don't get to ask, "Will I respond?"—for to ask that is already to have responded. Instead, with calls, as with life, there is no existential option to abstain. Staying in bed or putting on our hiking shoes—we make a choice either way. The decision that we must make is *how* to respond.

Calls are often missed when we confuse them for questions. We often simply attempt to "answer" the call. In this way, the call merely becomes a self-standing question, rather than the call putting *you into question as a self.*

See, the funny thing about a call is that it is always calls us to selfhood. Think about it.

What is the first thing that you say when you answer a phone, at least prior to caller ID? "Hello, this is Aaron." Or: "Aaron Simmons speaking." Or: "Aaron Simmons, how can I help you." We literally identify ourselves as the one to whom the call has been offered. Without such identification, think about how weird calls would be:

"Hello?"
"Hey!"
"What are you doing tonight?"
"I don't know yet. What about you?"
"It kinda depends on how much homework I have"
"Oh yeah."
"Yeah"
"Why is that?"

"Well, because my Philosophy professor is crazy and expects us to read like 100 pages of Levinas tonight."
"Seriously."
"Yep."
"Come on, Josh, just drop that course already?"
"Hunh?"
"Isn't this Josh?"
"No, this is Kate."
"Crap."
click

Notice that even in this call and response, what eventually gives context to the entire conversation—its meaning maker, if you will—is the moment of self-identification. Without that moment, the entire thing is ultimately silly and a cause of confusion.

Why is it that when we dial the wrong number we apologize to the person? Why not simply say, "Hey, it is great to meet you. If you live in Greenville, do you want to do something tonight?" Of course, the reason we don't is quite clear: we don't know who the caller is and they don't know who the called is. So, we're both unable to give any other sensible response to the call that's underway. Indeed, this is why, when we're on the receiving end, we can see that, even if the caller is anonymous, if we answer then we tend to be the ones who have to say who we are in order to see if the caller intended to call us or not.

So, calls not only call *to someone*. In particular, they call us *to be someone*.

Further, calls are always *from somewhere*. Their status as a call might depend on the response, but after having responded, then the call is seen to have preceded us. It is like Kierkegaard suggests, life is always to be lived forwards, but only ever understood backwards. In other words, I can't eliminate the risk of the next step before taking it. Only having moved can I ultimately tell whether I moved in the right direction.

I know that this sucks, or at least it easily can seem to, but it is the way things are. It is up to us whether we see it as a cause of resigned despair as we sigh and sink deeper into the lukewarm bathtub of the "they," or as a cause for courageous faithful action as we take up the task of selfhood as defined by risk with direction.

Often, we spend a lot of time worrying about the source of the call because it tells us not only a lot about the caller, but it also helps us to understand the appropriate decision that we should make in response.

Is it my mom calling?
Is it my ex?
Is it my next?

Perhaps the call to selfhood comes from God. Perhaps the call comes simply from some anonymous force of existence itself. Does it matter if we decide one way or another?

I will think more about God in the next chapter, but for now the point is that the deep stuff about who we are is connected most decidedly to what or who we name as calling us to ourselves.

What someone believes matters.

At the most basic level, what you believe about the source of your call to selfhood determines how you make sense of the status of yourself and others. *The stakes are high indeed.*

The point is that ideas have consequences and what we believe underlies what we do. But, this runs in reverse too. Actions give rise to ideas and what we do facilitates what beliefs we can take seriously as options. When we understand ourselves as responses to a call, we have work to do figuring out what or who calls, and how we decide will, in many ways, form the frame internal to which we then interpret ourselves.

T. S. Eliot said that we have to "prepare a face to meet the faces that you meet."[13] This is the challenge before all of us. Whether you take yourself to stand before God, an all pervasive life-force, or the anonymous void, or the crack in the wall that is a doorway to the "upside down" (yes, *Stranger Things*—unlike Radiohead, Megadeath, and coffee—is amazing), you have to realize that *you always stand before something*.

The call comes to us from somewhere—*or so we should choose to believe*. Otherwise, if there is no call, then we run the risk of thinking that there is no task of selfhood. If that is the case, then we simply are. I am a fan of existentialism, but I think Sartre was wrong about how he chose to make sense of himself and the source of freedom. The really important kind of freedom is not the existential agency that defines us no matter how we respond to the call to selfhood. Instead, I side with Aaron James regarding the importance of our decisions activating our freedom as a lived reality. Whether you stand with Sartre or James on this front, it matters that we can all move in different directions.

Wherever we stand,
it takes courage to stand,
somewhere,
on purpose.

Although I disagree with Sartre about the caller (he is trying faithfully to become an atheist, and I am trying, I hope faithfully, to

---

13   T.S. Eliot, "The Love Song of J. Alfred Prufrock," available at: https://www.poetryfoundation.org/poetrymagazine/poems/44212/the-love-song-of-j-alfred-prufrock. Accessed June 2, 2023.

become a Christian), I agree with him that we have to make the most of what has been made of us, and then, at every moment, to continue the process. In other words, as we have noted repeated on our "camping trip" together: *we are who we are becoming.* Our subjectivity is a task that requires us to live truly as we care about believing true things. To give up on truth is to give up on ourselves. A "post-truth" world, for what it is worth, is a world that has been abandoned to the assholes.

The call comes *to someone, from somewhere,* and is always calling *for something.*

Ah, so here is the difficult part, as if ethics and ontology were not hard enough. How do we know what the call says? What if you pick up the phone and the person speaking is using a language you do not understand?

Que faites-vous alors?

What if the person speaking is using words you understand but in ways you don't?

Wal-mart is pretty in the evening time after caterpillars march through cell phones.

What?!

See, the hermeneutic task returns over and over and over again! In one of my previous academic books, *God and the Other* (Simmons 2011), I develop this idea and call it a "recursive hermeneutics" in that the interpretive decision always recurs in light of the interpretive decisions we have made. Our choices frame what choices we are able to make and this continues for all of our life.

We not only decide *to* respond, not only do we decide *what or who* calls, but also we have to decide *what* the call says. I say we have to decide, rather than just to figure out (as I would do when asked a question), for a simple reason: almost nothing is obvious. The ass-hole will see others as in his way. The humble person will see others as opportunities for engagement. The success-minded person will view the world as task of external accomplishment. The faithful person will understand the world as the horizon of virtuous becoming. How we see things changes what is "there" for us to see. The "world" is not a collection of objects, but a horizon of meaning.

Let's formulate this in a phrase that will likely make sense to all of us (especially if you are a fan of old Twisted Sister videos):

What are you going to do with your life?

Is this phrase a question or a call?

Parents of my college students far too often give voice to this as a question. Moreover, they will usually think that this question should be met with an answer in relation to a job, preferably a very well paying and secure job with benefits. Of course, within our current economic framework, jobs matter, but when we are oriented toward faithfulness rather than success, jobs matter because they are specific ways in which we live out how we have chosen to hear the call to ourselves. When we think that we are "called" to a specific job, then we stop being selves and become employees. The key is to flip things such that we begin to see the call as a matter of what we take to be worthy of our finitude and then see the job as a particular manifestation of how we can make our practices align with that value-judgment. The job is secondary, the decision about meaning is foremost.

So, will you hear *"What are you going to do with your life?"* as a call (to selfhood) or merely as a question (about employment)? If it is the former, which I hope it is for you, then the point is that there may not be any precise answer that will suffice to quiet the continued questions from the crowd that continues to think jobs are definitive of dignity. Instead, with becoming there is only decision, and then more decision. But, and this is really, really cool: once the decision is made, then you get to "live forwards" in ways that might facilitate making different decisions as things develop.

We are who we are becoming.
We live forwards and understand backwards.
Risk remains, but direction always matters.

Life is, ultimately, all about owning up to the decision to become someone you like being (choosing faithfully to respond to the call), and then finding ways of doing stuff (like getting a job in order to answer the continued questions) that helps you to continue in that task of faithfulness at every moment. Faithfulness is not about how many trophies we have on the wall, or how many rejection letters we have in a drawer. It is all about who we are and what we value.

The goal is not to change the score, but to change the game.

My specifics are just that, specific to my case. Your specifics will be your own. I like riding mountains; you might like riding waves (both are awesome). I like tea; you might like coffee (you would be wrong!).

Our life story is effectively the account of how we responded to the call.

What is your story?

As for me, I started as a physics major, but thought my professor was strange. He had a pocket protector, always messed up buttoning his shirt, and had tape on his glasses. Yep, he was "that guy." So I went to Europe and fell in love with art and ideas, came back and went to graduate school to watch FSU football with the hope that I would become a professor so I could spend my summers fishing. Along the way I discovered that the questions keeping me up at night were questions worth spending my life asking. Philosophy let me do this so I decided to devote my life to becoming a philosopher. Here I am still trying to become one, deciding how to answer the call today, and tomorrow.

I could have chosen differently and things would have been ok— that is what I think too many people forget. Remember Heidegger's notion of "mineness" that we discussed earlier? Well, Kierkegaard actually introduced that basic idea long before Heidegger. In his early 20s, the young Kierkegaard realizes that it just doesn't matter if he ends up knowing everything about worldly success if he never discovers what is true "for him."

Kierkegaard's path was his. My path is mine. Your path is yours. Don't let your parents, your friends, your professors, or your pastors tell you what the right path is, though it is always a good thing to seek out the advice of such people who display wisdom, virtue, and humility. Those who seek faithfulness tend to gravitate toward others who do so also.

Only when you choose for yourself can you, then, and always after the fact, realize that the *question* "What are you going to do with your life?" was indeed a *call* that defined your life: *Who are you becoming?* Then you can see that what you thought was a term paper was really an invitation to a different identity; that joining this or that group was actually the turning point in everything that followed; that sometimes grabbing coffee with someone ends up being about much more than just coffee.

Sometimes just not being too busy is the key.

My vocational story about how I "found my calling," as it were, is a story about my becoming, but crucially (and thankfully!) *it is still ongoing*. I am still working on who I am and who I hope to become. I have not yet finished the story and so I am still trying to figure out whether some questions that I am trying to answer will turn out to have been calls. We will see.

So, let's get back to the childlike wisdom of Drake.

You thought I would forget? Drake is, though eminently forgettable as a "rapper," important to remember when considered phenomenologically.

"I know when that hotline bling, that can only mean one thing." (Drake 2016)

Notice that, for Drake, everything is clear from the outset. There is no reason to pick up the phone because we already know *who* is calling, *what* they want, and *why* they want to speak to us. In this way, Drake reduces the call to not much more than a *sigh*.

It's her again.

Sigh.

It's him again.

Sigh.

That sigh is what the indie rock band, Death Cab for Cutie, would call "the sound of settling."[14] Settling is, for Kierkegaard, termed "leveling." It is what happens when we no longer strive for meaning, but just settle for what "they" say. It is what occurs when we abandon the task of becoming and just "level" ourselves according to the standard of the "herd." We hear the voice of the "crowd," but at the cost of learning silence from the lilies and the birds. Our

---

14   Death Cab for Cutie, "The Sound of Settling," *Transatlanticism* (Barsuk Records, 2003).

cell phone never stops ringing and yet we never own up to the recursive hermeneutics of the call. We become sheep. Baaaaaaaa Baaaaaa. Sigh.

To avoid this settling, this leveling, then we must realize that when that hotline bling, it never, ever, only means *one* thing. It all depends on what you decide about *who* is calling, *what* they want, and *how you will* respond.

When we stop being overwhelmed by questions about success, we might begin to hear calls to faithfulness.

"It's him, again!"

Who am I?

"It's her, again!"

What should I do?

When we let the call be a call that truly calls us, then we might begin to see that the really, really great *callers* are those that are not immediately identified, because the lack of clarity invites us into a greater hospitality to the unexpected, a more profound willingness to imagine what is possible, and ultimately a greater desire for deeper relationships without setting preconditions for what they need to look like.

When we let the call *call us*, then we might begin to see that the really, really great calls are those that remain a bit perplexing because the mystery invites us to dig deeper. As with almost everything we have been talking about, this is not a one size fits all kind of thing. Mystery is always plural and dynamic. The mystery that calls one person might be the triviality that bores someone else.

For example, my wife loves beaches because she says that she never tires of looking into the infinity of the ocean, but for me beaches just all kinda look the same (and the hotels, crowds, and noise of the *they* almost always invade the existential aloneness that I so often seek). I love mountains because every trail, every tree, every rock, every part of it is different and opens onto new worlds. For my wife, as she never tires of telling me, the waterfalls and trails all kinda blend together. We see things differently, but encourage each other to keep seeing things that facilitate joy in light of the mysteries that show up in different ways for us.

In the same vein as John Muir's statement about hearing the call of the mountains, Henry David Thoreau (2006) claims that in order to go for a walk, you have to be willing to get lost. I think he is right. When the mountains call, they call us to a very long walk indeed. But here is the important part: *all calls do this.* Whatever calls you, it calls you to a life defined in response. We are all becoming someone, but we are not all doing so on purpose.

In this way, though I love Muir's sentiment, "The mountains are calling and I must go," I disagree with the specifics of his claim. Yes, we all must respond, but not all of us choose to "go."

Think about that Dr. Seuss book that spikes in sales around graduation time each spring, *Oh, the Places You'll Go.* We tend to narrate our lives as almost occurring out of necessity: *Here is where you will go, so get ready!* What if we changed the story of our lives to make it focus on the contingency, the fragility, and the risk involved: *There are lots of places you could go, but where do you think is worth going?*

As for my own story, I did the best I could to make the best decisions with the information that I had at the time, but the unmanageable persists and there is always more left to do. And so I did that again, and again, and again.

Somewhere along the way, my *sigh* at knowing that the call could only mean one thing, turned into a *self* whereby I realized that *there are always more options.*

I have enjoyed the journey, though on some days it is easier to keep moving forward than on others.

The important thing is to keep walking with Thoreau, to keep hiking with Muir, to keep camping with Kierkegaard . . . to keep responding . . . *faithfully.*

The mountains are calling . . .

I choose to go.
Come with me.

But, please, let's listen to something other than Drake on the way there.

8

Of God and Trout Fishing

I love God and I love trout fishing.

I readily acknowledge that any direct mentions of "God" can be risky. Since this whole book has been about risk with direction, maybe this is a risk worth taking. I have repeatedly noted that by "faithfulness" I do not mean "religion." Indeed, I have tried hard to make this entire book philosophically compelling regardless of one's determinate religious identity or lack thereof. As such, I have avoided talking much about God, even though we did see that part of the lesson of the lilies and the birds was figuring out what stands as "God" for us. Existentially, "God" can function as a term/idea that conveys David Foster Wallace's point about the necessity of worship and Kierkegaard's point about the inevitability of positioning something as ultimate.

And yet, in light of the different locations of mystery that we considered in the previous chapters, it is also important to realize that sometimes "God" can also be meaningfully deployed in specifically religious ways. That is what I am going to try to do in this chapter.

In light of the stupid polarization of our contemporary world, showing hospitality to people, and the views that they hold, is an important aspect of faithfulness as a way of life. That doesn't mean that we accept the views or agree with the positions, but it does mean that we work to pull back from the immediacy with which we declare people with whom we disagree to be either irrational or immoral. They might be wrong, but they probably have reasons for their views and consider themselves to be striving for virtue. Being misguided sucks, but it is rarely sufficient to be dismissive. Remember, ethical aloneness is impossible. Our finitude names not only our vulnerability, but also our relationality.

Going fishing with someone else is a great way to foreground the humanity that is shared in ways that might facilitate mitigating the disagreements and differences that remain in lots of other ways. So, in this chapter I invite you to go fishing with me and along the way, let's talk about God. My goal in this chapter is not to persuade you about any specific account of religious identity, belief, or practice. Instead, it is an opportunity for us to think together about ultimate directionality. I am not assuming that you will agree with me about God, but I do think that we can find common ground about the importance of hope.

Ok, let's set the drag on our reel and make a cast into the water. Maybe the fish will be biting today. Either way, I have sandwiches waiting in the cooler and look forward to the conversation on the river.

Hope, Desire, and Limiting Out

I don't know any trout fishers who don't hope to catch a bunch of fish. The specific goal is to "limit out"—or to catch the number of fish that you are legally allowed to keep, assuming that they are big enough—or "keepers"—in the first place. In fact, although now I pretty much only practice "catch and release" fishing, I still narrate my fishing trips in terms of "limiting out" or not. In this sense, it might seem that whether or not one was successful in the fishing trip depends upon whether the hope for catching fish comes to fruition as a successfully achieved object: the number of fish in your creel.

Viewing things this way forces an economic logic on a practice that I think resists such a framework. There is no exchange function in trout fishing so that you put in the time and energy and are reward- ed with the catch of the day and go home "successful." Instead, trout fishing is an activity that, in its very enactment, calls us further into such action. Catching fish simply invites a continued desire to keep fishing. Not catching fish invites the hope that the next cast changes your luck. Indeed, no one who has fished very much will find it strange to hear of someone who ended up staying on the river hours past when they planned to leave because they continued to live into the hope that "one more cast" will lead to the "monster brown" or "record brookie." Either way, whether at the end of the day you end up limiting out or going home empty handed, the reality is the same: *right now you are fishing*—your hope to catch fish is part of that present experience, but it is not ultimately what matters most.

Let me try to unpack this idea a bit more.

Although I hope to catch fish, it's also true that every minute spent fishing is already the actualization of the thing I really hope for: *to be able to spend time fishing*. Yet, precisely in the actualization of this hope, here and now, every minute spent fishing is itself also a moment of anticipation, of expectation, for the catch "yet to come" if I continue to fish.

In this way, trout fishing positions me in a rather odd temporal relationship to myself: I am already who I hope to be (namely, a person fishing) and yet who I am is not yet who I hope to become (namely, the person who has continued to fish—and who maybe catches some fish). I have already achieved that for which I hope and yet I am still living forward because of the continuation of the other side of the hope itself. My desire for the future catch is part of what it means to be fishing, and yet catching the fish furthers my desire to keep fishing.

This already/not yet structure is characteristic of what we might term an *eschatological* logic that, in its emphasis on faithfulness, stands opposed to the economic logic by which desire is officially terminated when the object of desire is successfully obtained.

I propose that such eschatological hope is part of what characterizes the "religious" as a category. If I am right about this, then it is hardly surprising that many have viewed the act of fishing and trout fishing, in particular, as a quasi-religious activity. I mean, watch *A River Runs Through It* and tell me that the religious rituals of the father are not manifest in the fishing rituals of the sons.

There is more than a passing resemblance between trout fishing and religion. There are special vests(ments) worn while engaging in the activity that distinguish you from those unaffiliated with the community, such as waders, boots, nets, creels, etc. Fishing, like religious devotion, takes long hours of ritualistic practice in order to achieve mastery. There are all sorts of sacred objects associated with the practice itself: the trout rod that your parent bought you years ago (and has now been broken and repaired repeatedly because now that your parent is no longer living the rod is something much, much more than a tool for catching fish), the fly or lure that has been passed down for generations (and that you will swear can enact miracles when everything else fails), and the lucky hat that is so worn that it barely stays on your head without the help of duct-tape (but somehow impacts the feeding patterns of trout to such a degree that if you forget it then you just might as well turn around and go home).

By the way, thank God for duct-tape!
And all the church said, "Amen!"

Further, there is a hidden wisdom handed over only to the initiated that continues to further one's role in the community: the secret "honey-hole" that only you and a few other people know about, or the fly or lure that works with particular trout on a specific stretch of river (for what it is worth, when fishing with my dad—who is no fan of fly fishing, but prefers ultralight spinning rods—I am partial to 1/8 oz brown rooster tails with silver blades).

Finally, trout fishing is something that is presented to others as an invitation to join the community if they commit themselves to the right dress, rituals, and wisdom. Indeed, the first time I took my son trout fishing, I presented it to him in very much this quasi-religious way: he was being invited into a liturgy that would connect him with his great-grandfather, his grandfather, his father, and eventually, hopefully, with his own children.[15]

Now, let me be clear that I do not want to get sidetracked into very important, but peripheral, debates about what counts as "religion" or not. Although there is a significant body of work in that area, and I have contributed to it elsewhere,[16] here I am content simply to note the plausible similarities between those cultural traditions that are historically termed "religions" and the specific practice of trout fishing. To that end, my use of the term "quasi-religious" is meant to be a vague descriptor that highlights trout fishing as an interesting phenomenological case-study, rather than a rigidly precise term indicating something sociologically significant about the "religion" of trout-fishing. Though from my experiences fishing in

---

15   I want to note that the gendered dynamics here are entirely contingent on the fact that I only have one child who happens to be a boy. None of what I am saying in this chapter should indicate any sort of gendered assumptions about the practice of fishing. Indeed, I think that resituating fishing in the way I propose here might invite us all to see it as connected to human existence, as such, in ways that productively challenge some of the sociological realities that too often attend the practice.
16   As one of the best recent philosophical discussions of this topic, see Schilbrack 2014. For my own contributions to these debates, see J. Aaron Simmons 2015, and 2023.

Tennessee and North Carolina, the disciples of that "religion" are numerous indeed!

The eschatological structure of hope and desire on display in trout fishing is distinct from the other modes of hope that tend to characterize our lives and our practices. I think that there are two primary modes that we more regularly navigate: *existentiell* and *existential* hope. For what it is worth, if these technical terms are off-putting to you, then just think about them as *objective* hope and *subjective* hope. That said, I am using these technical terms because I am trying to stay close to two philosophical resources that stand as the background for my account of these varieties of hope. In the first place, I am thinking about the broader distinction between existentiell and existential developed by Martin Heidegger (2010) in relation to the various ways that human existence is experienced. Additionally, I am building on Claude Romano's (2009 and 2014) notion of expectation as a phenomenological structure of lived experience. Romano's account is especially helpful because he suggests that there is an expectation proper to historical desire (the hope for a new phone, say) that is distinct from the expectation proper to historical beings capable of such desires (the hope that distinguishes beings like us from tables and shoelaces, for example).

What I am calling *existentiell (objective) hope* is the contingent temporal hope that we have for a specific possible future outcome. Maybe you hope for a new truck, a new dog, a new job, or a new dating relationship. The object doesn't matter as much as the orientation. Existentiell hope is *object*-oriented. Upon obtaining that suitable object, the hope disappears along with the desire for the hoped-for thing. Once I get the truck, the dog, the job, or the relationship, I am no longer defined by the hope for those objects because my desire has been fulfilled in the external achievement of them.

Interestingly, I take existentiell hope to be a mirror-phenomenon of fear. I find myself in a state of fear always only in relation to some specific future due to a discrete relationship to a threatening object or outcome: the snake in the grass, the bear in the forest, or the loss of some valued thing. Fear is overcome by existentiell hope insofar as such hope allows us to live toward a future in which the feared object/outcome is defeated by the obtainment of an object/outcome that we desire. Existentiell hope and fear are both characteristics of our being the sort of beings who stand in relation to external states of affairs that are affectively impactful on whom we are trying to become.

Existential (subjective) hope, alternatively, is the sort of hope that simply and necessarily accompanies the existence of finite beings like us. Insofar as we are temporal, hope attends our basic sense of the world and ourselves. We project ourselves into the future because we hope for the future itself. I admit that this abstract idea might sound weird, so let's see if we can make it a bit more concrete. We go to bed hoping for tomorrow, we brush our teeth because we expect that we will be alive for the coming weeks and months in which bad dental hygiene would come back to bite us.

In other words, existential hope is not the hope for a *particular* future, but for *the future, as such*. It is the way desire accompanies what it means to be temporally constituted. It is existential hope that allows history to be a space of expectation. In light of where I have been, I now hope to go someplace else. In this way, my present is constructed by the complicated tension of memory and expectation that defines the human condition *as historical*.

Accordingly, whereas existentiell hope was the inverse of fear, existential hope is a mirror-phenomenon of anxiety. Unlike fear, anxiety has no direct object, but simply attends our existence due to the vulnerability that defines it. I am not anxious about the snake in the grass or the loss of my job, I am anxious because I am a being defined by limitation and eventually death. So, in a technical sense, I am not anxious about dying (though I might fear death), but anxious because I only ever live as accompanied by the awareness of eventually dying.

Existential hope is what helps keep anxiety at bay, but it is only because we are beings who are threatened by anxiety that we are beings capable of existential hope. Existential hope and anxiety are phenomena that would be unintelligible to beings who live forever or are invulnerable. Yet, we are neither of those things and so our very being (and our becoming) is framed by the interplay between such hope and anxiety.

If existentiell hope is a matter of objective-obtainment (getting the car, or house, or job, etc.), existential hope is a matter of subjective-identity in so far as it structures my relationship to desire as an historical phenomenon.

That is a mouthful so see if this helps a bit. In existentially hoping for the future, as such, I name my present moment as defined by potentiality. Romano hits on this idea when he describes the sort of expectation attendant to existentiell hope as temporary—it passes into and out of existence as our desires emerge, get disappointed or fulfilled, and then get abandoned as we move on to new desired outcomes and objects. On this model of existentiell hope, we are, he says, "turned and directed toward the future,…to which a certain event, if it takes place, would correspond" (Romano 2009, p. 36). Alternatively, Romano notes that the sort of expectation that accompanies existential hope is that which is a "permanent" facet of human existence.

Importantly, existential hope is not able to stand on its own without existentiell hope. Existential hope without existentiell hope is too vague to be of much help when it comes to narrating our historical lives. It is a frame without content. The contingent objects of existentiell desire allow the necessity of existential hope to appear as a background condition, and yet the framework of existential hope is what makes any desire for a specific object possible for beings like us.

For example, I can only hope for the new car because I take myself to have a future, as such, in which the car could be obtained. Yet, only in hoping for the new car (or some other discrete object) can I give the future, as such, any concrete shape.

Whereas existential hope without the accompanying specificity of existentiell hope is empty, existentiell hope without the framework of existential hope is literally hopeless since there would be no "time" in which we could move into the future where our hopes could be, as Edmund Husserl would say, *fulfilled.*

Notice that both of these varieties of hope are matters of human meaning playing out in history. That is, they both function according to the "not yet" directionality of human striving. But, as we might be encouraged to ask by the lilies and the birds, what if history is not ultimate? Or, asked slightly differently, what if we are "already" what we are "not yet"? This is where we transition into the domain of eschatological hope.

Eschatological hope is what the philosopher, John Caputo (2015), calls "hope against hope." It is the hope that animates Viktor Frankl's account of living through the holocaust in *Man's Search for Meaning.* It is the hope that Kierkegaard discusses when he suggests that we are suspended above 70,000 fathoms and yet there find faith. This hope is neither a hope for some particular outcome, nor it is the hope that attends temporal existence, it is the hope that repositions history in relation to eternity such that the already/not yet comes into a lived tension right where we are. In such a relation, as C. S. Lewis says somewhere in *The Four Loves,* "all that is not eternal is eternally out of date."

The philosopher that I think has done more to position eschatological hope in the context of embodied religious existence is the French new phenomenologist that we have considered in previous chapters, Jean-Louis Chrétien (2002). Although Chrétien uses different terminology than I am proposing here, in his discussion of "the unhoped for," he is quite clearly presenting hope in the register that I have termed "eschatological."

His account of "the unhoped for" is complicated, but for our purposes here, we can understand it as that future that we think is largely impossible and so have no idea how we could achieve. Rather than our ordinary idea of hope being a matter of wishing for something to occur, Chrétien's conception is of hope as a rupture from all ordinary logics of achievement. Hope, he thinks, is not about the appropriate expectation that attends getting from here to there, but of living toward a future in relation to which we currently have no map. It is risking ourselves in a direction that seems to require more of us that we are able to imagine. In this way, then, "hope," he claims, "disassociates itself from all calculation" (Chrétien 2002, p. 104).

He details that this notion of the unhoped for is marked by its desire for what is ordinarily considered impossible—it is entirely cut off from the normal despair that attends the frustration of existentiell desire (when we don't get the car, the job, or the house). Chrétien admits that such a strange form of hope is "wholly other than [what] most people hope" because it ruptures the calculation by which we so often understand finite value in a transactional world. I would rephrase what he is saying here as follows: *In a world defined by success, living faithfully is viewed as strange behavior indeed.*

Eschatological hope, or the unhoped for, when taken up in ordinary ways in daily life, is a matter of non-economically relating to the eternal significance of each moment, rather than being defined by an economic evaluation of this moment's instrumental importance to a particular future that we desire. "The *unhoped for*," Chrétien continues, "is what transcends all our expectations, and the inaccessible is that to which no path takes us, whether it is one that is already traced or one that we project in thought" (2002, p. 105).

I love the way that Chrétien expresses this point because it gets at the heart of the already/not yet structure I am describing. The unhoped for is not some-*thing*, but it is the depth dimension at play in relation to a God for whom all things are possible. "Biblical

124

hope," Chrétien explains, "has as its object what can be hoped for only from God, thus what is impossible by any human force, and what we neither could nor would have to hope for from ourselves and by ourselves" (2002, pp. 107-108).

There is an old saying that one never stands so tall as when falling on one's knees. This is exactly right—as we discussed earlier in a secular tone regarding the hard work of humility. Chrétien's (2000) account of prayer as a "wounded word" beautifully captures this idea. He claims that the phenomenon of prayer humbles us (even in our embodied posture) because it exposes us to what we cannot fully grasp, imagine, or circumscribe. Yet, it also elevates us by positioning us in relation to the transcendent. God meets us in prayer, Chrétien suggests, because there we also meet ourselves as humbly standing before-God.

Now, whether or not you identify as "religious," I think we can all learn something from Chrétien here because it is in such statements that he strikes me as a trout fisherman. To go trout fishing requires that we embrace humility at the very same instant that we express hospitality to that which is bigger than us. Not being humbled by mountains and rivers can lead to devastation. Only by appreciating one's insignificance in comparison with them can one faithfully navigate them with appropriate respect. Yet, doing so occasions an understanding of selfhood as not merely a matter of natural processes, causal relationships, or financial status.

Having tripped many times while wading through a rough patch of whitewater, I have fallen frequently on my knees (and ripped many pairs of waders in the process). In those moments when the immediacy of embodied vulnerability was all too humbling, as is also the case with prayer, I better appreciated the surprising dignity of the human condition.

Here we stand as always already flawed, finite, and fallible, *and yet we are so much more.*

It is when the waters threaten to overwhelm me that I get a glimpse of what it means to approach selfhood as a faithful task of constant becoming. To illustrate this point, listen to Chrétien's description of what is involved in hoping for the unhoped for:

> [These] two seemingly inverse movements—humiliation and uplifting, dejection and exaltation—constitute the space in which the unhoped for is received: together they signify that the unhoped for is not and cannot be our work, they recognize and confess its excessive character. And the thought of the unhoped for goes together with the thought of humility. (2002, p. 108)

Eschatological hope maintains our desire (whether religious or quasi-religious) because it refuses finality. Fishing fosters the desire to keep fishing, prayer fosters the desire to keep praying, living fosters the desire to keep living. All three are oriented toward a seemingly impossible goal of finishing what constitutively remains open. Again, though, with God all things are possible. In relation to God, we already are the selves what we are never quite yet able to be on our own.

Here and now I am a fisherman, but only by continuing to desire to go fishing will I continue to become a fisherman.

I should note that existentiell hope without eschatological hope risks being defined by achievement, rather than defining what achievements are worth seeking. Being open to eschatological hope helps us avoid the distorted worldview so very common in our asshole-laden world whereby people matter more because of their nationality, their citizenship, their prosperity, etc.

Alternatively, existential hope without eschatological hope risks being future-oriented without ever having a meaningful vision of the future. Being open to eschatological hope, thus, also helps us to avoid wandering aimlessly. Getting lost is very different from going hiking, even if going hiking requires that we be willing to risk getting lost.

Ultimately, eschatological hope allows us to appreciate both existentiell and existential hope as crucial aspects of our embodied existence as a matter of faithfulness. This shift from the economic logic of success to the eschatological logic of faithfulness is the key to appreciating the "religious" dynamics in play in my love of God and in my love of trout fishing. In order to fill in this idea a bit more, let's look at Kierkegaard's account of the knight of faith as an example of what such faithful living into eschatological hope might involve.

The Failure of Success: Kierkegaard on Faithfulness
Although Kierkegaard is almost ubiquitously associated with a philosophical consideration of faith, his most sustained consideration of faith, as recounted by the pseudonym Johannes de Silentio in *Fear and Trembling* (1983), is anything but straightforward.

A quick explanatory note here may be helpful: Kierkegaard often wrote under pseudonyms in order to explore various modes of existence from inside of different subjective perspectives. In this way, he doesn't pretend to be objective, but instead admits that we always navigate the world from within a variety of embodied practices, cultural assumptions, and personal beliefs. In this way, he displays an awareness of the recursive hermeneutics we discussed earlier. So, in this discussion here I will refer to Silentio as the author since it allows us to remember that we always speak from somewhere. Philosophy is not primarily about objective certainty, but instead emphasizes the importance of subjective investment.

Fear and Trembling is a text notorious for its layered presentation and lack of hermeneutic clarity. Indeed, what else would we expect from an author whose name indicates that he isn't able to say anything. Indeed, the text is literally written by a guy named John of Silence (I always thought "Silent John" was a bit more badass sounding though). Although the interpretive options attending this text are myriad, whatever else it is, it is a text that attempts to define "faith" and then present a lived example of what such faith would look like in practice.

The "knight of faith" is an honorific that Silentio applies to Abraham, but also, and perhaps more interestingly, uses as a phrase to indicate a way of life or mode of existence that is not an historical relic, but a contemporary possibility. Consider the following account in which Silentio imagines running into the knight of faith on the street:

> The instant I first lay eyes on [the knight of faith], I set him apart at once; I jump back, clap my hands, and say half aloud, "Good Lord, is this the man, is this really the one—he looks just like a tax collector!" But this is indeed the one. I move a little closer to him, watch his slightest movement to see if it reveals a bit of heterogeneous optical telegraphy from the infinite, a glance, a facial expression, a gesture, a sadness, a smile that would betray the infinite in its heterogeneity with the finite. No! I examine his figure from top to toe to see if there may be a crack through which the infinite would peek. No! He is solid all the way through. His stance? It is vigorous, belongs entirely to finitude: no spruced-up burgher walking out to Fresberg on a Sunday afternoon treads the earth more solidly. He belongs entirely to the world...He finds pleasure in everything...He attends to his job...He goes to church...He takes a walk to the woods...Toward evening, he goes home, and his gait is as steady as a postman's. On the way, he thinks that his wife surely will have a special hot meal for him when he comes home—for example, roast lamb's head with vegetables...His wife does not have it—curiously enough, he is just the same. (Kierkegaard 1983, pp. 38-39)

Here we see a variety of important dynamics that characterize the life of faith.

First, faith does not get reflected in an external transformation. The knight of faith is indistinguishable from the tax collector—that is, he could be anyone: you, me, the old lady down the street, the dude at the DMV, etc. There is nothing about the knight of faith that allows for external recognition. It's like the ancient Buddhist instruction:

Before enlightenment, chop wood, carry water.
After enlightenment, chop wood, carry water.

Faithfulness, Silentio indicates, is not about external status, but about internal orientation. As Silentio notes, "he is solid all the way through." Unlike the literary narrative of Moses' encounter with God that left him literally glowing and his transformation visible from a far distance (Exodus 34: 29-35), the knight of faith is able to get lost in the crowd, as it were, precisely because faithfulness is not a matter of popular applause and brand recognition.

Second, Silentio stresses the surprising fact that the knight of faith "belongs entirely to the world." This is striking because we often think that a life of faithfulness will become fairly detached from earthly concerns in order to set one's gaze on the eternal.

For example, in my own Pentecostal tradition, we used to say of people that they were "so heavenly minded that they were of no earthly good." In other words, their "faith" led them to be so "holy" that they were unable to get their hands dirty in the messiness of the human condition. I am sure you know these sorts of folks. Rather than "finding pleasure in everything," as does the knight of faith, they find everything to be a distraction from what "really matters"—but in doing so, they lose sight of the truly meaningful. Religion becomes their sole focus and faith, for them, names a rejection of worldly living. These folks are often recognizable because they always have a critical word on their lips and a judging look in their eye. They take themselves to be so religiously virtuous that they alone know what is right.

Those people suck.

Importantly, Silentio does not allow faith to slide into such detached resentment. Instead, it is presented more like what one finds in C. S. Lewis' (2015) imaginative picture of the heaven (the eschaton) in *The Great Divorce*. Therein, Lewis suggests that far from heaven being a rejection of worldly embodiment, it actually signifies as a glorification and deepening of such embodiment. The grass is greener, the sky is bluer, the water is wetter, the mountains are higher. The eschatological experience is more—rather than less—embodied. In this way, Lewis invites us to entertain the possibility that redemption is not really about an escape from the human condition, but instead is about a decisive plunge into what it means for that condition to be seen "as good" by God (see Genesis 1:10, 12, 18, 21, 25, and 31).

For what it is worth, when I read books like *The Great Divorce*, it comes as no surprise to me that Lewis liked to hike.

In Silentio's account of lived faith, we are presented with a nondescript, unremarkable, and decidedly worldly individual. And yet, the faithful person is entirely different from the others.

Faith changes everything.

The knight of faith is somehow able to avoid giving in to the overwhelming temptation to hopelessness (due to the mundane reality of his job, his church, and the day in, day out routine of his life) and is somehow unaffected when his desire (for roast lamb) is thwarted by the cold reality of leftovers. As my wife can tell you, I hate leftovers. Clearly, I have not quite figured out faithfulness when it comes to what is for dinner.

This inner transformation that leads the knight of faith to embrace his or her existence as an occasion of joy (rather than refusing it in escapist rejection or in nihilistic denial) highlights the dynamics of eschatological hope.

Simply put, the knight of faith's identity is not defined by success, but by faithfulness.

As we have seen repeatedly as we camp together with Kierkegaard, faithfulness is not about having or obtaining or being something, but rather is about continually becoming what already critically defines your identity as directed beyond itself.

For example, I can be a successful swimmer by winning a swim meet, or a successful entrepreneur by founding a company and expanding it until a very lucrative exit, but I cannot be a successful father or husband in the same way because what it means to be invested in my son or wife is to be continually directed toward becoming ever more faithful to them. Faithfulness is about continuing in a direction that matters. Success is about reaching the end of the road in order then to change direction.

As Silentio notes, the knight of faith "is continually making the movement of infinity, but he does it with such precision and assurance that he continually gets finitude out of it" (Kierkegaard 1983, p. 41). And as such, as I often point out, he is able to "express the sublime in the pedestrian" (Kierkegaard 1983, p. 41). Silentio shows that faith is not about a specific outcome, or that faithfulness is a matter of existentiell hope. Moreover, he demonstrates that faith does not maintain temporality as an ultimate horizon, such that faithfulness would be a matter of existentiell hope.

Instead, Kierkegaard, via the perspective offered by Silentio, invites us to be transformed by the example of the knight of faith as we learn that faith is a revision of how history itself signifies as non-ultimate.

Temporality is ruptured by eternality in order that the eternal signifies as temporally significant, and does so *at every moment*. This is why the knight of faith can attend to his job, go to church, take walks in the woods, and navigate the commonplace realities of social life while still somehow finding "pleasure in everything." Faithfulness is a matter of eschatological hope insofar as it is a "task for a whole lifetime" (Kierkegaard 1983, p. 7). It reminds us that we have more work to do and that such work is worth doing. However, faithfulness also lets us see that if we think that we could eventually be done with the world, we would never have begun appropriately living in it in the first place.

Drawing on Silentio's discussion of the knight of faith invites us to see how thinking about faithfulness as the lived outcome of eschatological hope allows us to understand how the knight of faith can be "just the same" even though his specific desires for external achievements might not come to pass as he (existentielly) hoped they would. It is important that Silentio qualifies this description with the words, "curiously enough." In doing so, he acknowledges the way that the knight of faith has existentiell hopes, but yet is not defined by them. He is "just the same" because he is *already* what he hoped to be: faithful. Nonetheless, he is *not yet* finished with becoming faithful because a task for a lifetime is not something that admits of historical finality.

A God Who Goes Fishing
Whenever I feel hopeless, I go trout fishing.

I go fishing because it reminds me where my hope really lies. It connects me to the idea that the eternal is not somewhere else, but is performed in how we inhabit temporality. In this way, trout fishing helps me to see religious life as something that invites joy at every moment, despite the frequent disappointments that attend finitude, instead of something that defers joy as an external object only to be obtained "when this life is o'er," as the old hymn says.[17] Trout fishing signals that the religious goal should not be to "fly away," but to cast the fly into just the right spot here and now. Trout fishing helps me live into the fact that God is invested in our lives, and not just

---

17   "I'll Fly Away," lyrics and music by Albert E. Brumley (1929).

concerned about a possible after-life. If God cares about where we are now, we should too.

That said, like the knight of faith's relation to the roast lamb, I do desire to limit out on trout, but if I don't catch anything, curiously enough, I am just the same.

Well, at least I try to be.

The difficulty of faithfulness is not allowing it to be just a matter of expressed commitment, but instead always positioning it as a lived orientation. Similarly, even though I do hope to spend eternity with God—whatever that involves—such that I can sing "Hallelujah, by and by," I think that Emmanuel Levinas was right to say that we would likely only be worthy of the coming Messiah if we were to live as if the Messiah were never going to come (Levinas 1985, p. 114).

The point is that we must already be who we are trying to become; we can't wait until later to start becoming who we want to be because as the singer Donovan Woods rightly says, "there ain't no next year."[18]

Too many of us live today only in light of "next year." We constantly say that "next year" I will take time to fish. "Next year" I will get to the mountains. "Next year" I will spend more time with my family. "Next year" I will make joy a priority. But this way of living will always leave us depressed, disappointed, and despairing. What we do today shapes what "next year" will look like and so even though we have so many hopes for "next year," next year never seems to come. As we already learned, the "if only, then I'll . . ." is a logic that will rob you not only of your todays, but also of your tomorrows.

The goal, as Kierkegaard, Chrétien, and trout fishers all so profoundly

---

18   Donovan Woods, "Next Year," *Both Ways* (Meant Well, 2018).

help us to understand is to make "next year" unfold in light of "here and now."

I go fishing in order to be someone who continues to go fishing—catching fish is a nice side-benefit, but not the main/ultimate goal.

C. S. Lewis says somewhere that joy is found in desiring—this is exactly right when it comes to existentiell hope. Lewis recognizes that when we desire an object, the obtainment of that object often leaves us cold and without a good sense of how to move forward since our prior existence was narrated by the desire that no longer signifies. Yet, in eschatological hope, our desire is never exhausted because it is not about having/being/achieving, but about continuing to become faithful. Our desire is, instead, to grow in faithfulness. And, as Kierkegaard reminds us so very often: becoming a self is not something that you finish like a jigsaw puzzle that can be framed and put on the wall, but an ongoing response to a compelling mystery that calls us to respond.

There are surely other activities that invite us toward eschatological hope, but for me trout fishing is distinctive for two reasons. First, it invites me to become who I already am, and to desire that which is *already* the case and somehow remains *not yet* finished. Second, it anchors me in the idea of *kenosis*, or a form of humility as an emptying out, as key to lived faithfulness.

We already saw in Chrétien how hoping for the unhoped for brings humility and exaltation together. This kenotic framework is profoundly on display in trout fishing. Trout fishing is an essentially humbling activity because no matter how good you are at it, you are keenly aware that many of the aspects that make the activity possible lie decidedly beyond your control: the river flow, the fish behavior, the weather, hatch patterns, and the stream access, etc.

To go trout fishing is to abandon the idea of self-sufficiency. It is to embrace the notion that you don't control what awaits you at home for dinner, in a manner of speaking. But, at the very same time, it calls us to be ourselves because the decision that I do control is what facilitates any possible outcome: what fly or lure to use, which weight of line, whether to present the fly from upstream or downstream, and so on.

Religious life, like trout fishing, is about faithfulness as an investment in what we think matters. Yet, it is only in our enactment of the investment, the affective embrace of its contingency, that the meaning becomes activated. It is by going fishing that I can really say that fishing matters. I take my son fishing not primarily to give him the experience of catching fish, but in order to have a relationship with him in which we fish. The same, I think, is true in our relation to God.

Nietzsche claims that he could never get on board with a God who didn't laugh. Well, I want a God who goes fishing. For what it is worth, I think that the fact that Jesus was a fisherman is perhaps the greatest apologetic for Christianity! Sure, his being a carpenter is also good as a statement about not getting deceived by social status, but his being a fisherman is key to the lives we are supposed to live.

As such, I think that philosophers of religion would do well to move from a phenomenology of *religious* life (Heidegger) to a phenomenology of a *reel*igious life as exemplified by the narrative of Christ, expressed in Kierkegaard's notion of faithful living, and explained in Chrétien's account of the unhoped for.

A phenomenology of *reel*igious life encourages us to:

> Keep fishing.
> Keep praying.
> Keep being who you are becoming.
> Desire that which is eternally actual in order to transform historical possibility.

In other words, this phenomenology encourages us to have enough hope to keep hoping.

I want to conclude this chapter by turning to Anne Lamott, from whom one of the epigraphs to this book is taken. In her book, *Almost Everything: Notes on Hope*, she closes the book by saying:

> We have all we need to come through. Against all odds, no matter what we've lost, no matter what messes we've made over time, no matter how dark the night, we offer and are offered kindness, soul, light, and food, which create breath and spaciousness, which create hope, sufficient unto the day. (2009, p. 189)

I love this. Lamott rightly notes that we already have all we need for the journey, and yet we are not yet where we are going. The kenotic logic of eschatological hope is on display as she encourages us to take solace, but still to keep working.

In the end, no matter what I do while fishing, there is peace to be found in the fact that the river remains constant even as the water flows past me. It is already here and has not yet arrived. This dynamic relationship with the river offers a temporal reminder of what eschatological hope is all about. When we strive to become faithful instead of seeking to be a success, we imitate a God who kenotically meets us where we are and then invites us onward and upward, rather than a God who tells us that if we just do this or that, then we will be perfect enough to meet the divine.

This is a God that I can take seriously because it is a God who is trouble for assholes. This is a God who is trouble for our pretensions to certainty. This is a God who is unimpressed by our bank accounts, our Instagram followers, our degrees, and, yes, even our religious "holiness."

This is a God who goes fishing and invites us to grab our rod and come along.

Count me in.

9

ODE TO NIETZSCHE:
ON RANDOM IDEAS AND FALSE STARTS

One of the characteristics of Nietzsche's mature authorship, in addition to his abandonment of the Schopenhauerian nihilism and intoxication with Richard Wagner, was his aphoristic writing style. He eventually wrote like this because it allowed him to reflect his bodily movement. An avid hiker, Nietzsche escaped to the mountains not only for the solace and reflective intensity that it occasioned, but because his serious health problems didn't plague him as much when he was in the high country. The fresh air, the physical exertion, and the adventure all merged into an experience that provided health to him in body and mind. As a result, he no longer wrote in ways that are appropriate to long hours spent in the libraries (which Emerson said were filled with meek young people who are afraid of the risks of actual existence), but instead in ways that are better suited for the stops and starts of a hiker hardened by the necessities of steep climbs, rocky descents, brutal winters, and unforgiving isolation. Short bursts of activity followed by pauses and frequent shifts of direction became definitive of his later work and there is something about this I find compelling as not only a guide for writing, but maybe for living as well.

Thinking well requires time, nuance, and care, but stagnation can sometimes set in as we persist in trying to find a way to argue a particular point. Or worse, we begin to realize that our initial claim may no longer be as strong as we originally thought and yet we are so far in that we just push through rather than turning around. Nietzsche's insights on this front stem, in part, from Emerson's idea that a "foolish consistency is the hobgoblin of little minds" (1981, p. 145).

Emerson wasn't suggesting that we abandon all concern for coherence in our thinking, but instead reminding us, as we saw earlier, that humility and hospitality require us to be flexible in ways that might be frustrating if our goal is singularly to complete a project (success) rather than to strive for truth and excellence even if that requires revision (faithfulness). Emerson gives a nice image of what this approach to thinking and living is like. He says it is like the track of a sailboat across the ocean. If we look at the route from 30,000 feet, say, it may look like a straight line, but if we zoom in, then we can see that it is constantly moving back and forth in order to keep the wind in its sails. The same might be true of apps that track hikes or bike rides. What if we write in a way that reflects this embodied motion? Back and forth, but onwards and upwards. Or, as C.S. Lewis might say, further up and further in.

Maybe by writing in aphorisms Nietzsche understood what now underlies our culture's obsession with short impressionistic comments via TikTok. My son is currently 13 and he loves the "shorts" that pop up on YouTube because they "get to the point," as he says. I admit that my philosophical heart cringes at his distaste for long books and slow movies, but the hiker in me gets it. Perhaps even more so, the mountain biker in me does.

When you mountain bike, you spend a long time getting to the top of the mountain then to spend a relatively short time riding down it. Yes, the climb up is the price you pay to play on the descent, but when it comes to the mountain biking videos on YouTube, there are very few that record the hour-long climb. Rather, all that we get to see is the five-minute descent.

Aphorisms are like this. They help us remember why we came out here to the mountains in the first place. Yes, we still have to climb. But it is also ok sometimes to admit that climbs suck and that if we only ever climbed nobody would get into mountain biking. The same is true with thinking and writing. Yes, we still must think carefully and slowly. But it is also ok to present the thesis without the full argument in order to stimulate others to think with you, rather than simply check the work of your thinking for precision, completeness, and logical rigor.

To that end, in this chapter, I offer something of an ode to Nietzsche by writing in the style that he chose for himself. There are drawbacks in this style, but there are also distinct joys that it makes available.

☙

Sometimes when the sun hits the mountains just right, it looks like fog. At other times, the fog prevents you from seeing the mountains. Either way, the mountains remain.

☙

Good hot tea and dark chocolate are sometimes all that is required for joy.

☙

The cabin where I go to write has floors made of wood from the trees removed from the lot where the cabin was built. This gets Derridean deconstruction just right. When we cut down things to build something else, there is always something of what was removed that remains in the core of what gets made. What is true for these wood floors is also true for ideas and ideologies.

☙

I have always found it strange that professors make their classrooms as stressful as possible for exams. We listen to music because it changes our attitude and soothes our soul (King David understood this), so why not let the students listen to music? We go to the mountains or the beaches because stress is not simply mental, it is physical. We should let students take their tests wherever they want. Worries about cheating just reveal our failure to create a culture in which trust is prized as a virtue.

∽

I like dogwood trees because they have a tendency to grow in the most unexpected places. In the early Spring, they make their presence known when everything else is still hiding.

∽

I fully endorse the musician Andrew W.K.'s idea of partying hard. I don't see it as an encouragement to drug-use and frat-house behavior. Instead, I see it as a quasi-Stoic conception of living life without regret. Indeed, Seneca (2018) compellingly suggests that when we prepare for death we learn to live. Partying hard is the notion that we should not half-ass our way through life. Or, as Big Daddy Kane would say, when it comes to faithful living, there "ain't no half steppin."[19] Thoreau's idea that we would come to the end of our life and realize that we had not yet lived is terrifying. It reflects the life of someone who skipped the party and yet still has to clean up the mess. I once had some students who decided that philosophy should be understood as "one big important party." I think they are right.

∽

---

19 Big Daddy Kane, "Ain't No Half-Steppin," on *Long Live the Kane* (Cold Chillin' Records, 1988).

Sometimes I just don't know how to pray. I should probably restate that as "I *often* don't know how to pray." When those times occur it is not because I don't know if God exists, but instead I just think that there are always more important things that God should be attending to than what I am praying about. Right now I am praying that my parents are able to close on their new house and every time I try to pray about it, I see the faces of the people suffering in the war in Ukraine. I then find myself saying, "Help them in Ukraine, God, I guess we are ok." But, that period at the end is where I am brought to grief. It really should be a question mark. "I guess we are ok?" It is as if I am asking God to help me realize that I don't need to worry about what is in front of me. Maybe this is all a mistake because prayer is always personal? Chrétien says that prayer is a wounded word and it ruptures our sense of self-sufficiency. So, maybe prayer is not so much *personal* as it is the challenge to my *personality* as definitive of moral value? The questions continue . . . but so do my prayers. Maybe we all would do better to have more question marks than periods in our prayers?

෴

Leaves give our ears the ability to hear the wind, but they prevent our eyes from seeing very far.

෴

When off-roading, dropping your tire pressure makes a big difference in both traction and comfort. Continuing to drive forward on rough ground in the same way that we do on smooth pavement just leads to a sore back and a stuck truck. Taking the time to let out some air before leaving the pavement is an important way to ensure that you can make it back home before it gets dark. What is true in this case for trucks is also true for our lives.

෴

Mountain Laurel blossoms prove that individual beauty is not erased in the context of community, but rather fostered by it.

❧

I prefer mountains to beaches, but both convey the same sense of horizonal infinity. They allow us to see as far as is possible and yet remind us that we can't see everything. Kant called this "the sublime" because in our very awareness of inadequacy we are emboldened in the amazing thought that we can do so very much.

❧

My grandma raised me to love sweet tea—one cup of sugar per gallon was the exactly right proportion. But, now in my 40s, I can't handle that much sugar so I have trained myself to drink unsweetened iced tea. I acknowledge that this would be viewed as a moral failure by my grandma. I have discovered that if you put enough lemon in it, it tastes pretty darn good. These days, every time I drink iced tea I think of the ways in which we get so used to things one way that we assume it is the *only* way things could be. Sadly, too many folks take for granted that *their* way of looking at things is simply the way things are. Maybe they should drink some unsweetened tea more often and, in the process, interrupt their assumptions about value.

❧

It is said that the early bird gets the worm, well the early mountain biker gets spiderwebs in the face.

❧

Sometimes we have to cut down trees to see the view. Other times, we destroy the view by cutting down trees. Simone de Beauvoir was right about the ambiguity of ethics.

ↄ

The day that you take out a life insurance policy is a weird one. On that day you enact the fact of your own death and yet also mark the continued concern for those who will go on living.

ↄ

When the fog is especially low, climbing to the mountain tops is the only way to see anything clearly.

ↄ

Wearing body armor, knee pads, a helmet, and gloves while mountain biking is not to prevent crashes, but to prepare for them. The same is true in life.

ↄ

The fact that Limp Bizkit is popular again just shows that the absurdists were on to something.

ↄ

I was recently sitting on top of a mountain overlook working on this book and a woman came up to me and after a few pleasantries I told her about the book I was writing. She proceeded to tell me that she grew up biking and hiking the Sierra Nevada range in California. Then she recounted a tale about a time that she "almost died" while biking with folks that were better than her. On one section of the trail she got scared and instead of stopping and walking her bike down, which she should have done, she didn't want them to think badly of her so she rode the section in terror. She explained that she probably would have been fine had she believed in herself and ridden with confidence, but instead she got hesitant and so things went badly. As she walked off, she said to me: "Hesitancy

143

will get you killed in the mountains." She is right. Humility is virtuous because it keeps us from doing what we shouldn't. Hesitancy is vicious because it causes us to think mediocrity will facilitate excellence.

∾

We would be wrong to miss some of the lessons that COVID taught us:

1. The "office" doesn't have to be *at the office*. For example, Zoom allow us now to realized that mountaintops are great places to hold "office-hours."
2. A "bro-nod" is as effective as a handshake for greeting people, and a heck of a lot safer.
3. "Don't forget to wash your hands" counts as moral wisdom.

∾

Don't go for the bunny-hop off the boulder if you don't have money to pay for a new wheel when you case the rocks at the bottom. In other words, risk requires preparation.

∾

Knee pads and full-face helmets illustrate that the contingency of our existence is marked by our embodied vulnerability.

∾

We live in a society where mediocrity gets rewarded as excellence, excellence is mocked as a waste of time, kindness is disregarded in the name of success, and bullies almost always get the microphones. This reality has a lot to do with why I mountain bike. You can't be an influencer when it comes to rocks. You can't bully a tree into getting out of your way. You definitely can't feel big by making others feel small. The jumps, drops, skinnies, and wall-rides will level all egos. On the trails, humility goes hand in hand with confidence, and hospitality to others is simply part of what it means to share the trail. Maybe if more of us went mountain biking, we would learn to be better humans.

∽

My dad is currently sitting in the room with me as I write this. There will be a time when he will be gone. For now, that he is here is sufficient.

10

The Other Side of the Mountain

We spent a chapter focusing on Drake, who I really can't stand, so let's start off this final chapter by thinking about a musician I love: Ben Folds. On his track, "Still Fighting It," he claims that "It sucks to grow up, but everybody does."[20] When it comes to the guiding question of "What is worthy of your finitude?", I think that Ben Folds is on to something.

The philosophical point that Ben Folds gets right can be expressed this way:

Every trip to the mountains eventually requires going back to the truck and heading home.

Indeed, Ram Dass claims that when it is all said and done, we are all just walking each other home.

Well, let's think together a bit about "growing up" and the trip "home."

---

20   Ben Folds, "Still Fighting It," on *Rockin' the Suburbs* (Epic Records, 2001).

Today I am the oldest I have ever been. So are you.

I just turned 46, so does that mean that I am "over the hill"?

If so, what hill is that, exactly? If mountain biking is any indication, then the downhill stretch is where all the fun is.

Recently, I spent a week biking at Snowshoe Mountain Bike Park in West Virginia and then a few weeks later spent another week biking at Beech Mountain Bike Park in North Carolina. Both were amazing because the parks are full of extremely difficult (and fast!) downhill trails. They both have plenty of gnarly stuff, but after each run down the mountain, you just have to throw your bike on the ski lift and ride back to the top in order to hop on the bike and ride down again! Bike parks like these offer all the fun without any of the work. Life doesn't seem to unfold this way very often, though.

Just like my normal riding in Pisgah National Forest, life requires that you have to "earn" the downhills. Like growing up, climbs usually suck, but upon reflection, they are an essential part of the fun.

I remember when I was about 10 that my mom had her 40th birthday. It was a Wednesday. Don't be super impressed that I know that—it is because the party for her was after mid-week church. At her party there were lots of black balloons, a big sign that said "Lordy, Lordy, Kathy's 40!" and banners that said "Over the Hill!," and, for some reason that I still don't entirely understand, a huge stuffed vulture sitting on the table next to the cake. I guess the vulture was meant to signify that she was so old that it was only a matter of time before the vultures came to pick her bones? If I am right, that is quite a Kafkaesque gesture for a church birthday party!

I don't remember any other of my mother's birthdays and I don't really know why that party stands out so clearly in my memory. But it does. I mean, I even remember that I was wearing a blue shirt with yellow writing on it!

I had not thought much about my mom's 40th birthday for a long time until, about six years ago, I turned 40 myself. There were no black balloons, no sign saying "Lordy, Lordy, Aaron's 40!" and no vulture, thank goodness. Sorry, Kafka. Instead, it was a lovely evening at a local taco shop eating and talking with my wife, my son, and just a few good friends.

Turning 40 wasn't all that troubling to me, but then a few months later, my wife turned 40, and that was super weird. I kept trying to get my mind around the fact that I was married to a 40-year-old! That's as old as my mom! Sheesh. It just keeps getting stranger, by the way—now my wife, Vanessa, is older than her mom was when Vanessa and I got married! When did we get so old, or at least so much *older*?

I once asked my grandma what it felt like to turn 80 and, without missing a beat, she said that it felt exactly like turning 18 except that her body didn't work so well anymore. What she was illustrating for me was an idea that I could conceptually grasp, but didn't really understand until I began to live it for myself. Here's the thing: *you never really "feel" old*. You always feel like . . . well, *you*. But how old are we in that self-conception? I used to wonder whether, when people die, if they are always that age in heaven. That seems entirely wrong to me—being an infant for eternity, or being always "over the hill" etc. And yet, what would it mean to think about ourselves as some particular age forever? Which age would that be? Maybe we get to choose?

Imagine it: "Welcome to heaven, nice streets, huh? Like the gold? Master P helped us with the design. By the way, how old would you like to be for the rest of eternity?"

For my part, I think I would pick something like 28. Seems old enough not to be "too young" and yet not yet crossing that threshold of middle age, which does seem to set in somewhere in your 30s.

The idea of our self-conception having an age is a complicated matter. It would make for a cool short story to write about a person who somehow got lost in the mountains and spent a decade without encountering anyone else. Let's also assume that this person didn't have any ability to see their reflection during that time. If that person then made their way back to a city, would they recognize themselves in the mirror having aged 10 years? Would they find it odd that other people interact with them in ways that seem more appropriate for interacting with someone much older than they understand themselves to be? (Maybe this is what Nietzsche was trying to think through when he conjured up Zarathustra?)

My mom is now almost 80 and she says that now, when she looks in the mirror, she sees an old woman and it freaks her out.

Aging is frequently disorienting because we are vulnerable bodies. Our flesh not only marks time, but also carries it.

It is often said that youth is wasted on the young, but we might counter that experiential wisdom is reserved for those who make it to old age. Alfred Lord Tennyson grasped this point when he noted that "old age hath yet his honour and his toil" and then goes on to proclaim that even though "death closes all" that "something ere the end, some work of noble note, may yet be done" (1958, p. 67). Getting old is wrongly understood if it is framed in terms of loss, though aging does force us to grow accustomed, however uncomfortably, to lots of loss. Instead, getting old should be understood as a matter of realizing that life requires us to appreciate the different stages and contours of faithfulness as an embodied task.

I earlier referred to Kate Bush, but maybe we should spend a bit more time thinking with her. She famously claims to be "running up that hill." Here Bush is developing a point that is strikingly similar to the young Kierkegaard, who, when looking at his future with the boldness of anticipation, claims that it is "uphill that we are struggling" (Kierkegaard 1996, p. 38).

149

Is life really a hill? If so, then Kierkegaard seems to have a better sense of hiking than Bush. *Running* up hills usually leads to early exhaustion. *Struggling* up hills means that we adapt appropriately to what the terrain calls for. Maybe youth is wasted on the young because they have the ability to run further up the hill than the old, but often lack the wisdom to realize that their abilities are not unlimited. It takes age and experience to realize that slowing down a bit might mean that you can push further into the evening and sleep with more miles under your belt for the day.

In fact, I recently went mountain biking with one of my students. He is a competitive enduro racer and so on every single downhill run he left me in the dust, but on the uphill climbs he repeatedly charged ahead yet quickly ran out of steam. I passed him on every climb and by the end of the day he was cramping badly and struggling to keep going at all. We ended up cutting the day quite short because he was so worn out. He will easily beat me in any enduro race, but when it comes to *enduring* all that the mountain has to offer, a different pace and plan is required. Maybe my age helps me have just a bit better sense of the importance of having energy left for the late day climbs. Regardless of who you are, though, the longer you have ridden, the more difficult things become. Even the downhills, themselves, like at Snowshoe, are more dangerous late in the day because your legs are not "fresh" and your arms are starting to wear out.

Thinking about aging is only honestly done if, in the process, we think about death.

Attempting to cultivate faithfulness as a way of life requires that we also understand that even if the human condition is not something to try to escape, it is not permanent. Impermanence is ultimately the upshot of the human condition itself.

All hikes come to an end.
Camping trips don't last forever.

The amazing downhill bike run always ultimately heads back to the lot where you parked.
Eventually we have to pack up our fishing rods and make dinner.

A significant part of heading to the mountains is doing so in a way that allows us to get back down the mountain when it is time to come home. Struggling up the hill is a purposive act, but so is getting back down it. Whether we find ourselves running up the hill out of youthful exuberance, or reflective excitement, or in an adrenaline filled emergency situation, it is always much, much more dangerous to run *down* the hill. Few folks get injured hiking, or riding, uphill. Lots get hurt on the downhill section. Gravity almost always makes us go faster than we probably should.

In fact, I recently saw a shirt at a bike shop that simply said "gravity sucks." That shirt makes the same point as Ben Fold's song. Biking seems like it would be awesome without gravity, but notice that without gravity there can be no traction. Living seems like it would be awesome without growing up, but notice that without growing up, we would never understand life as a task of becoming.

That said, as we think about navigating gravity, hiking and biking are importantly different. When biking, the downhill is when all your senses are on high alert, you notice everything and try to put yourself on the right "line" to navigate the obstacles without injury. However, when it comes to hiking, going downhill is tricky because it is when we are the least attentive to the trail. The excitement of the climb is over, we already have the pictures from the scenic overlook at the top, and so we are no longer adaptively attuned in ways that facilitate responsible decisions. Judgment is always cloudy after a long day of exertion. Yet, if we have developed wisdom and learned from experience, then we might borrow from Dave Egger's poetic expression and realize that the task is to go "up the mountain, coming down slowly" (2004, p. 141).

Egger's phrasing here wrecks me every time I read it, but it is especially heavy on my mind every time I begin the descent back home from the mountains. When camping I always want to slow down the moments of the last night around the fire. When hiking I always want to slow down and appreciate the trees, flowers, and rocks the closer that I get to my truck. When biking I always want to go a bit more slowly on the last climb in order to keep the final descent in front of me as long as possible.

As we age, we become aware more and more that we are no longer running up the hill, but running out of time.

Oh, wow, look at that metaphor that I just used without really thinking it through. Notice that here my metaphor of "running out of time" begins to betray the economic logic of the success mindset that faithfulness should help us to resist. Running out of time is a phrase that presents time as a commodity; something that we "have," that we can "lose," and that we can "waste." But what if time is not a commodity, but the lived context in which meaning is made.

It is this sense of time that I hope has been conveyed in our guiding question for this book: *What is worthy of your finitude?*

Finitude is both the reason for the human condition's impermanence and also the condition of finding meaning as human beings. But time is not a thing like money, cars, and trophies. It is not something that we can show to others as a sign of our significance. It is, instead, the great equalizer. It is not something that we possess, but something that possesses us. Time is not "ours," but instead we *are* temporal.

Philosophers have long understood that death is not just the end of life, but part of what provides the depth dimension of life itself.

Plato describes philosophy as being preparation for death. Perhaps a better way to express his point is to say that philosophy is a sustained attempt to learn how to live. Yet, such learning is only possible internal to the limitations of life itself. If we were immortal, then we would also have more time to learn anything and everything. We could always put it off until tomorrow. As finite, we are only able to learn things during the short window between birth and death. So, we have to get busy, today, here, now, because tomorrow may never come. As we have learned from Donovan Woods, "there ain't no next year."

But, even if we grasp this sense of urgency, we might still ask: What does it mean to learn to live?

Well, for Plato, and for Socrates who serves as the main character in all of Plato's *Dialogues*, learning to live means seeking the good, the true, and the beautiful. It means to run after them, whether it involves going uphill or not, as the ultimate objects of our desire. Plato, here, lays out a general idea that gets picked up in various ways by Aristotle, Augustine, and even Derrida: desire shapes our identity. What we love reveals who we are. So, learning to love the good, the true, and the beautiful is the race we run as finite beings. Philosophy is the way we train for this particular race.

However, loving something indicates that we still don't fully possess it. I love what always lies just beyond my full grasp. Hence, the continuation of the desire for it. Accordingly, the good, the true, and the beautiful are not objects that I can be successful at "having." They are directions worthy of my lived risk. Faith means continuing to pursue what matters. Life, faithfully undertaken, is a race that we have to keep running so long as we are alive. Death ends the race, but it does so without naming anyone a winner. The award ceremony, as it were, is something left to be conducted by those who remain . . . those who are inspired to keep running ever more faithfully by having witnessed others a little farther down the trail who modeled running.

When it comes to awards for faithfulness, the recognition is not for successfully beating others, but for running well.

Philosophy is preparation for death insofar as life is something we learn by continuing to live today as faithfully as we can.

Plato calls to us all to:

Be reflective.
Be awake.
Be attuned.
Be purposive.
Be philosophers.

Whatever we do for a living, living should be what we do. Philosophy is the name that Plato gives to the committed investment to doing life well.

Maybe Plato was the inspiration for L.L. Cool J's lyric: "doin it, and doin it, and doin it well"?[21]

Let's consider just a couple other philosophical accounts of the role of death in life.

Martin Heidegger suggests that part of what it is to be a being like us—that is, a being who asks questions about existence and wrestles with whether life has meaning—is to exist in light of death. There are, obviously, lots of ways that such existence might unfold, but for Heidegger it is important to be "authentic" in our relation to life, death, and ourselves. Such authenticity requires that we work through our own deaths as not just possibilities out there somewhere, but as actualities that temporally determine the meaning of our everyday lives. We are not just beings who will eventually die, Heidegger claims. Instead, we are, each and every one of us, *being-toward-death*.

As I wrote the previous sentence, I got a text from my wife informing me that a young girl (8th grade) at my son's middle school had

---

21   LL Cool J., "Doin It," on *Mr. Smith*, Def Jam, 1995.

committed suicide today. I am heartbroken. My son didn't know her personally, but regardless, his world makes a little less sense today than it did yesterday. How do I talk to him about this? What good is the philosophy of death when it comes to our actual encounter with finitude in ways that are simply too heavy for us? Right at this very moment, I am not sure I have an answer to that question.

And yet, maybe this sense of being broken, being inadequate to the task, is Heidegger's very point. What I mean is that, for Heidegger, being-toward-death is not some morbid thought, but simply who we are.

We are existentially constituted—whatever the direction of our lived risk—by finitude. As traumatic, senseless, and I would say, radically evil (in the sense that there is no final justification that makes it all ok), as that young girl's suicide is, the tragic thing is not that she died—again, we all do—but that she died before she learned to live; before she even got the chance to. It is *that fact* that, right here, right now, makes me so angry. I am crushed and trying to find the words to say to my son because I want him to know that it is ok not to have answers, not to understand, not to think that it all works out in the end. It might not.

That particular existential risk is one that we all must find ways to navigate, to live in light of. In that sense, death seems to cast an especially dark shadow over our lives. But, again, Heidegger's point continues to resound: Death is not something we would be better without. Without the fact of death, of finitude, of aging, of vulnerability, of limitation, we would not be us.

If all downhill trails were accessible by ski-lifts, then we might get really good at riding the gnar, as it were, but it would come at a striking cost to our cardio health. Ski-lifts are awesome, but they are designed for vacations. Everyday life is a matter of climbs and downhill runs. One without the other is either all work or all play. We need both.

I know some of you might think that this is some typical clap-trap existentialism that tries to convince us all to embrace suffering and, like Westley from *The Princess Bride*, realize that "life is pain, princess, and anyone who says differently is selling something."[22] Maybe rather than doing philosophy and seeking faithfulness oriented toward the good, the true, and the beautiful, we should just paint our fingernails black, put on dark eyeshadow, and listen to The Cure.

Although I do like The Cure and I don't really have any issues with "Goth" culture one way or another, this interpretation would be a drastic misunderstanding of Heidegger. *Existentialism, importantly, is not just for goth-kids.*

Being-toward-death occasions authentic existence by positioning us as able to see life as a matter of risky decision. Though I disagree with Camus and Seneca that suicide is just one more option for our existential freedom, I think that they, like Heidegger, rightly understand that decisions are risky only if death is an actuality for us. Life has significance and value precisely because it is fragile.

The logic of success tries to deny the reality of death by implicitly implying that if we can just do, have, and accomplish enough that we can somehow overcome the human condition. But, that is backwards. The human condition calls us to realize that no matter how much we do, have, or accomplish, we are still *being-toward-death.*

"Authenticity" is a complicated and problematic idea in existentialism, but for our purposes I think it is a good synonym for being adaptively attuned to our embodied situation. Authenticity operates according to the logic of faithfulness because it does not deny risk, but faces up to it, navigates it so far as possible, and embraces it as necessary for joy.

---

22   William Goldman, *The Princess Bride*, Shooting Script, 1987, available at: https://www.dailyscript.com/scripts/princess_bride.html

Remember the lilies and the birds. Silence, obedience, and joy . . . *ultimately*.

Sometimes that joy feels so very impossible. As it does right now as I think about that young girl in my son's class. Being-toward-death is not a disguised theodicy, or intellectual justification of evil in the name of some eventual good. The idea of joy . . . ultimately, is *not* that eventually there will necessarily be joy that somehow erases the pain. As Lorna Shore reminds us, the pain remains. But it need not have the final word. That is where the hard part of faithfulness comes in—choosing to keep moving when it seems so hard to take the next step. It is when I think about just sitting down and giving up that I think about Sisyphus and his rock. Camus was right to say that we must imagine Sisyphus happy. He had his rock, and therefore he had his roll—that is, he had his purpose. He was never going to finish pushing the rock, but so long as he lived, he had a direction in which to move.

We do too.

In those moments, we need to remember that we are not on the trail of life by ourselves. As I explained earlier, empirical aloneness is often something to seek out in order to refocus our attention, but ethical aloneness is an impossibility. We are inherently relational. We are always walking, hiking, biking, fishing, and camping with others. Who you walk with matters. No one needs friends like Job. But, we all, like Job, need friends. We need someone who stands as an encouragement and an example to us in those moments when we feel most threatened by despair. When being over-the-hill seems like a good reason just to give up, we need others who show us that often the best trails are located on the other side of the mountain. They teach us to go up the mountain, but also to come down slowly.

What is the name of that person for you?

For me, his name is David Kangas. I mentioned him earlier, but let me tell you more about him.

David Kangas was one of my professors at Florida State University when I was a graduate student there, prior to going to Vanderbilt University to work with another David (Wood). David was the first person who really invited me to go camping with Kierkegaard. David was a philosopher, but he was also a hiker, a climber, and a man in love with mountains.

On January 9, 2013, also a Wednesday, I received the following email from David, forwarded by a mutual friend to a group of us who had been his students:

First off, "stage 4" cancer, which is what I have, is by definition incurable. So treatments are a matter of buying time. How much time is, of course, unknowable by anyone. I'll take whatever becomes available.

The treatment protocol will be something like the following: first, radiation to the head to reduce/eliminate the tumors in my brain. Second, IF I have a specific genetic mutation, something they are still figuring out, I can begin taking a pill fairly immediately to start targeting the tumors in my lungs. If I don't have the specific mutation, then it will be a normal regimen of chemo. Treatments will happen probably at UCSF and here in Turlock and will pro-ceed over the course of the next few months.

Given my overall good health going into this, the doctor seems to envision that I may have some time, time enough to go back to teaching in the fall, for example. We'll just have to see, but I would certainly look forward to a good summer and fall of fairly normal activity--teaching, writing, climbing, being with family, etc. That would be wonderful.

Existentially, I consider myself fortunate to have never believed the human condition was "curable" (the professional opinion of a phi-losopher which I couldn't resist telling the doc). Nor, thankfully, have I ever put much credence in the techno-pragmatic complexes of our culture, never having believed that the human condition was a "problem" to which the proper techniques of management are to be found. Mind you, I WILL let the technicians do with me what they will and can! But in the end there is the unmanageable and we would be trivial beings without it.

So, onward with my day!

I have read these words more times than I can remember. Every time that I do, I am inspired—in the etymological sense of receiving breath. David's words, as such a perfect reflection of his life, give me the breath I need to keep moving, to keep hiking, to keep riding, to keep living even as being-toward death. Well, not just "even as" but exactly because of! Notice that in these few paragraphs David does not evade the fragility of his embodiment and he directly confronts the reality of his situation. He notes that his prognosis is not just grim, but "by definition incurable." As such, his treatments are not going to change his situation, but they might "buy time."

There it is again: time as a commodity. But, immediately David refuses to allow the success logic to take hold. "I'll take whatever becomes available." Like the person who has learned ethics on the trail, he displays *humility* about the unknowability of how much time remains, *hospitality* for however much there is, and *gratitude* for it all.

Running through the treatment protocol, David tacitly acknowl-edges that once we figure out what is worthy of our finitude, the rest is simply logistics.

Again, expressing the gratitude that characterizes faithfulness as a way of life, David notes the contingency and uncertainty that accompanies all of our situations. How much time does he have?

How much time do any of us have? "We'll just have to see," he claims. This is not an expression of resignation and despair, but rather of anticipation and hope: "I would certainly look forward to a good summer and fall of fairly normal activity--teaching, writing, climbing, being with family, etc. That would be wonderful."

Yes, yes it would be. It would be wonderful no matter what lies ahead. The focus on the present, not in denial about what is going to come, but in open-eyed awareness that the ultimate decision is what to do with today such that our hopes for tomorrow might be fostered as real possibilities. His summer and fall of "fairly normal activity" is predicated not only on what happens with his cancer, but what he chooses to do with whatever time he has. It will be wonderful only if he continues to live his life as wonder-full. Not unimportantly, Aristotle says that philosophy begins in wonder. Well, for David, and all who seek faithfulness rather than success, life always occurs in wonder too.

Always the consummate philosopher and teacher, David then turns from a focus on his own existence to the existential condition that he shares with all of us. "Existentially," he writes, "I consider myself fortunate to have never believed the human condition was "curable" (the professional opinion of a philosopher which I couldn't resist telling the doc)." Here while being told by his doctor that he was going to die, David responds by reminding the doctor that we always were going to die. Being-toward-death is not a curse, even if it is often so very hard to accept. It is the condition of everything that matters to us. On a long enough timeline, all physicians will fail to keep their patients alive. So much for "success," I guess. But, while we are alive, thankfully there are doctors of philosophy who help us to avoid the temptation to think that the final goal is not-dying. Instead, as we learned while walking with Thoreau, hiking with Derrida, and biking with Plato, and camping with Kierkegaard, the task is to learn to live before we die.

In contrast to the logic of success, which always thinks that more stuff can solve our problems, David positions himself as "never having believed that the human condition was a "problem" to which the proper techniques of management are to be found."

Boom.
Suck it, assholes (and accountants, administrators, and actuaries)!

Importantly, though, living a life oriented toward becoming faithful does not mean that being successful is impossible in all respects. Logistics matter and so David does not allow us to get lost in abstraction: "Mind you, I WILL let the technicians do with me what they will and can!" I love this point because he seems to think that his readers, his students, his friends are likely to misunderstand that philosophy is not a detachment from living but a fuller investment in it. Thank God and science for vaccines that are "successful" at preventing severe diseases. Thankfully even if physicians can't cure us of the human condition, they can make that condition a bit more enjoyable by fixing broken bones, providing antibiotics, and performing surgeries.

We should be grateful that even if trauma is real, so is therapy.

And then David, who eventually passed away in 2016, writes the line that in many ways has caused me to rethink how I live, the direction of my risk, and my approach to aging and death: "But in the end there is the unmanageable and we would be trivial beings without it."

If someone asked what it means to camp with Kierkegaard, this sentence is what I would say in response.

The logic of success always eventually ends in the reality of failure. The logic of faithfulness always acknowledges risk (the unmanageable), but it also affirms that "we would be trivial beings" if that risk were not essential to our lived condition.

Aging is hard. Death is scarry. Life is risky. And yet, choice remains.

I hope against hope that by seeking faithfulness as a way of life, I will be able to say, faithfully, when faced with death: "Onward with my day!"

That exclamation point.
Wow.

I may have never biked in Whistler, but since I started writing this book, I now bike regularly in Pisgah National Forest, feel comfortable on most black diamonds at Snowshoe Bike Park, both of which are a huge step up from what I was doing just a few years ago, and occasionally I am able to convince my son to go riding with me. I still have not fished in Alaska, but I now sponsor a trout fishing club at my university and still hit the rivers with my dad whenever I can. Offroading in Moab remains yet to do, but I have spent more time off road in my truck in the past three years than I have in all of my previous 43 years. I still haven't kayaked class 5+ whitewater, but I did buy my wife a paddleboard and we regularly go together to Lake Jocassee, which is crystal clear and surrounded by mountains.

The point is that what matters in my life is not checking boxes of accomplishments, but spending every day in a way that is worthy of my finitude. Yes, I still have to go to meetings, I still have to grade papers, I still have to pay bills, and I still have to navigate a world that is marked increasingly by political division, conspiracy theories, and assholery.

It is crucial that we realize that faithfulness is not escapism. It is investment in full awareness that the way things are is often not how they have to be. Our choices matter and so, in faith, I will do my best to continue striving toward the good, the true, and the beautiful even if I am never "successful" in arriving at any of them. I hope that you will do your best to do the same whether you are still figuring out how to make it up that hill, or you are on the other side of the mountain trying to learn how to come down slowly.

Whichever direction you decide to orient your risk, don't forget that sometimes going camping with Kierkegaard is a good idea for us all . . . whatever age we are in heaven.

Whatever you decide to do with your finitude, however you narrate what is worthy of your life, be sure to grab your helmet and gloves and then *Just Send It!*

You got this. I will see you on the trails.

Postscript
Embers, Like Mountains, Remain

It has been a great day in the mountains and now I am back at camp. The fire is in that early stage when the flames are flickering and yet might still fizzle out and require rekindling. The bikes are dirty and show the signs of having navigated some of the best miles of gnar in Pisgah: Avery Creek, Black Mountain, and Bennett Gap. Thankfully, my body is without any serious injury—just a few bruises on my shins from where the screws on the flat pedals got me.

There are a bunch of good feelings in life, but one of the very best is the exhaustion that comes after a long day of physical exertion in the course of doing what you love. I used to get a faint shadow of that feeling when I worked construction in high-school and college. After a full day of painting door frames, hanging sheetrock, or sanding trim in preparation of the primer coat, my body was always weary, but in that "good" way that makes you feel like your time was worth the effort. There is an important difference between that feeling at the end of a day of construction and a day of being in the mountains. While on the construction site, I felt good that the day was done, whereas when I am in the mountains, I feel good that I am there, at that moment, and that more such days constitute the hope for tomorrow.

Today two friends and I rode Avery Creek, which is a Pisgah black diamond rated trail. This trail definitely warrants its black rating. It has sizable drops, steep rock gardens, big gap jumps, and a lot of technical flow. It reminds you that risk is real in mountain biking, as in life.

The thing that really hits me, though, as I unpack some gear from my truck in preparation for making dinner, is that the downhill run (which seems to go on forever and causes your quads and forearms to really remind you of your embodied vulnerability!) was only possible because of the extremely long climb to get to the trailhead. All the way up Clawhammer road (which isn't much of a road, but more of a dirt/gravel assent through the mountains), then when you get to the top you have to "hike a bike" up the trail known as "Upper Upper Black" because it is so steep and rocky that there is almost no way to ride up it (well at least not for me). After miles of climbing your bike up steep trails, then more miles of carrying your bike up steeper trails, only then do you get to tighten your helmet, put on your elbow guards, zip up your body armor and "drop in" so that you can "send it" on the downhill. Although the risk greatly increases going down, it is only by willfully, intentionally, purposefully directing yourself uphill for a very long time that the downhill is "earned." It is not the downhill run that justifies the "good exhaustion" back at the campsite, it is the climb that preceded it.

The same is true of nearly all other outdoor activities. Backpacking always leaves me "good exhausted" because to get to the really cool campsites you have to traverse many miles before even getting the opportunity to make camp. But, then, sitting around that small campfire eating food out of a bag that was reconstituted with water filtered from the nearby stream and then boiled over an ultralight campstove, your body reminds you why this is all so very worthy of your finitude.

Nothing tastes better than hot chocolate around the campfire after a 15-mile day of backpacking. It is as if your body enacts the "yes-saying" that Nietzsche claims is the condition of real living and that Derrida claims to be included in the welcome of deconstruction.

Yes.
Yes.
So much yes.

The climb, the miles, the strenuous hike—they are all part of what makes this day the day that it is. It is the exertion then that now warrants the laughter with friends by the fire, the taste of the food eaten with long spoons, and the heavy rest that comes when in a sleeping bag with stars above.

While riding a different trail recently, Sycamore Cove, one of my good friends and frequent riding partners, Seth, was crossing a small (and narrow) wooden bridge (imagine three foot boards laid to facilitate crossing a small waterfall that runs beneath the trail, not something with handrails and opportunities for good pictures), when he was brought face to face with his vulnerability. It had been raining a lot in the days prior to our ride and, although we had made sure that the trail was dry enough to justify riding it (riding extremely wet trails is bad form because it causes damage to them), the wooden boards of that small bridge were just wet enough to cause his back tire to slip out from under him when he gave a small pedal-stroke in order to reposition his front wheel to miss a bit of the trail that had washed out. Life is ultimately a game of inches, and seconds. That almost imperceptible flick of the pedal caused the back tire to slip, the front tire to miss where he was trying to place it, and over he went . . . down into the ditch created by the long years of that small waterfall running over the landscape.

I was riding behind him and all I heard was him yell in panic and then he was simply gone. Seth is well over six feet tall and when his bike slid off the side, he disappeared with it. Then, silence. I went racing up to the spot, jumped off my bike and ran to where he had gone over. There, on the ground, with his bike a couple feet from him, was Seth. He had missed the rocks, which were scattered all around him. He had missed the downed trees from storms long passed. He had landed in mud. He was fine. He was also lucky.

The hip hop group, Mobb Deep, has a track called "Shook Ones." Well, that day, Seth and I were both "shook." It could have gone so very badly. He and I both attribute his safety to my lucky bright yellow Wu-Tang socks that I often wear while riding new trails. But, although it could have gone badly, it didn't. There in that mud, Seth took a deep breath and felt the contingency of his existence, and yet he and I both appreciated the beauty of that very contingency. Gratitude was the air we breathed.

We didn't have to be there. You don't have to be where you are. None of us have to be directed as we currently are.

Philosophers have long expressed the wonder that comes with this awareness of the beauty of the contingency of existence by asking "why is there something rather than nothing?" There are lots of answers that various philosophers have given to this complicated question, but for me, sitting here by the fire thinking about that close-call, and about the fact that Seth and I were back on the trails just a few days later hitting even bigger features and pushing each other to find joy in the fragile moments of finite existence, I am less concerned with the answer to "why there is something" and more impressed by the fact that we, you, me, are all part of the something that is.

Good exhaustion is not only occasioned by the steep climbs, but it is also conditioned by the fact that we could have been doing something else. We could have been sitting on the couch all day. We could have been in the hospital with a loved one. We could have been stuck at the office. We could have been rained out and unable to get to the trails. But here we are. Tired, yes, but in all the right ways. Tired because we are not invulnerable. Tired because we are not infinite. Tired because we . . . simply are.

The fire took. It is now ready for me to add larger logs so that it will burn long into the night. This fire will be the focal point for the conversations to come, the locus for the fellowship that is so life giving, and the source of the warmth that belies the dropping temperatures here in the mountains.

My son, Atticus, loves campfires. He loves them so much that they are often the source of great frustration when we camp together because I am always nervous that he is going to burn down the forest. He just wants to play with sticks in the fire all night long. He especially likes to burn the end of a stick and then blow out the flame on the stick so that the back bit at the end of the stick can then be used to write on nearby rocks.

The tricky thing about Atticus's love of campfires is that he lacks the experience with them that provides the practical wisdom about how to navigate them responsibly. Fires have a way of refusing to go out easily. They deceive even the wisest among us.

My dad, who has spent a great deal of time in the outdoors since he was a child, recently had a fire in his backyard firepit. It was a lovely evening of hotdogs and smores with family and then, as the night ended, he poured water over it and went to bed. The next day, he went to clear out the ash and remains from the fire the night before and so took a shovel and scooped out what he assumed was the, now cold, charred pieces of wood. He threw the shovel's contents into the woods behind his house and cleaned up the last few remnants of the grandkids inability to keep all the graham crackers in their mouths and went inside. About fifteen minutes later he happened to glance out of his window and, to his horror, saw that the ground where he had thrown the remains of the previous evening's fire was now, itself, ablaze!

The embers down deep in the firepit had somehow avoided the water that he poured over the night before and had remained hot.

They remained ready to reignite. Simply put, despite his best efforts to eliminate them, they remained.

Embers are like that. They stay warm long after the flames go out.

Thankfully, my dad was able to grab the hose and douse the new fire in his backyard. But, believe me when I tell you that he stood there a long time spraying water on everything.

The fire in front of me now is burning brightly, but unless I really make sure to "drown" the fire before going to bed, the embers are likely still to be hot in the morning even though the fire itself has been out for hours.

Fire safety not withstanding, I think that there is an important lesson that we can learn from the embers that remain. This is a lesson that I think can speak to us all as we close out our time in the mountains together. The idea is that our lives should be more like embers than fires; more like mountains than cities. Fires come and go, but embers remain hot long after the fire is gone. Cities come and go, and so does the cultural relevance of this or that particular important thing celebrated by influencers within the cities, but the mountains that we see in the distance remain stable even as our fashions, our priorities, and our life stages change.

I am now 46, but can still go to the same spot that my dad and I fished together when I was 20. It remains there as a witness to the fungibility of my own interests. The river doesn't care if I fish it or not, but I care if I don't teach my son to fish.

I am now a Full Professor of philosophy, but I can still go to the same trail that I hiked when I was a grad student wondering if I would ever even find a job. The mountain doesn't care if I return, but I love that my life can be marked by miles on the trail as much as by career accomplishments.

My wife and I have been married for over 20 years and yet the place where we went camping together on that first date so long ago remains. The trees have grown and generations of animals have come and gone there in those forest. The forest doesn't care if we go camping again, but my wife and I definitely find peace in the fact that in the face of so much that is lost as we age, that place stands as a testament to our investment in each other.

Embers, like mountains, remain and they call out to us for a response.

The first rule of being in the mountains is to "leave no trace," but when it comes to human existence the opposite is true. Yes, we are vulnerable, but we are also relational. These are the two facts about the human condition that I have argued motivate the need for faithfulness as a way of life.

What will remain of what you have willed to be true, to be meaningful, to be beautiful in the world?

There are two ways to think about the "traces" that we leave of our finitude. We can simply make a *mark*, or we can leave a *legacy*.

Making a mark is fine, but it is also fleeting because it operates according to the logic of success. It is what happens when you donate money to get your name on the plaque outside a building, or endow a scholarship that then carries your name, or do something that causes a statue of you to be built in the local park. These are all good things and many of us have benefited from the "marks" made by others.

Leaving a legacy, by contrast, appeals to the logic of faithfulness. It is not about your name being remembered, but about others being able to live into their own names in light of the virtue, the excellence, and the example that you made plausible as a way of life worthy of undertaking.

Marks are like fires. Fires burn brightly. Plaques shine in the sun. Fires crackle and pop and make their presence known. Praise from others is easy to see and the applause from the crowd is easy to here. Fires are a record of our activities in real time. Marks are things that we get to see as part of our own experience.

Legacies, alternatively, are like embers and mountains. Mountains can often disappear into the background and be forgotten in light of the new housing development, the outdoor shops, the new cars and new phones that occupy our attention. Embers can be forgotten as we pack up the truck, thinking that what really mattered is now finished. Similarly, legacies are not things that are shiny and popular. They are the record of long persistence. They are mementos to the importance of making meaning, not just cheering what the crowd thinks matters.

Marks can disappear once the plaque is changed, the statue breaks, and the scholarship expires. Legacies remain even if their origins are forgotten.

I care far less that my son wants to "be like me," than I do that he wants to be kind, charitable, and courageous. Those virtues are what matter. Accordingly, I try to live a life that leaves a legacy such that those virtues are normative for him. They are habits that he simply lives into, rather than objects that he desires to obtain.

A life of faithfulness leaves a legacy worthy of our finitude. Rather than encouraging others to be "like us," faithful legacies foster space for others to be faithful to what they think matters. It is not about getting others to remember us, but to remember why it matters to live on purpose. It is not about being celebrated as having won the game of life, but about appreciating every day what Nick Riggle (2022) terms "this beauty."

This beauty of existence.
This beauty that we are here.

This beauty of good exhaustion.
This beauty of those who have walked the trails before us, like David Kangas, and now form the cloud of witnesses encouraging us to keep moving forward.

This fire is beautiful, but the embers that remain hot tomorrow will remind us that tomorrow is beautiful too, even if the fire is gone. Life is poorly understood according to a success logic of achievement, but it shines forth in its contingent singularly when we enact a faithfulness logic of ever striving toward who we hope to become.

I am stoked that my buddies and I made it safely down Avery Creek today, but the accomplishment that matters is not that we rode that trail, but that we prioritize riding as part of our lives. I want to catch the trophy trout, but what matters is not that I have a fish on the wall, but the eschatological hope that motivates me to keep fishing.

Though it is cool to make the mark of getting your name on the list of folks who thru-hiked the Appalachian Trail, it is much cooler to leave the legacy whereby others (who may never even hear your name) live into joy and find agency in their spheres of influence.

Embers, like mountains, remain. As vulnerable and relational beings trying to figure out what is worthy of our finitude, that stability should humble us and yet inspire us toward an ever deeper gratitude.

Thank you for joining me on the trail, for hiking with me a few miles more, for casting out your line into waters in which we both stand, for dropping in at the top and fist-bumping me at the bottom, and for coming camping with me . . . and Kierkegaard.

Our time together has been so very worthy of my finitude.
I hope it was worthy of yours as well.

REFERENCES

Arendt, Hannah. 1968. *The Origins of Totalitarianism, new edition.* Orlando: Harcourt, Inc.

Beauvoir, Simone de. 1976. *The Ethics of Ambiguity.* Trans. Bernard Frechtman. New York, NY: Citadel Press.

Bonhoeffer, Dietrich. 1954. *Life Together.* Trans. John W. Doberstein. San Francisco, CA: HarperSanFrancisco.

Buber, Martin. 1970. *I and Thou.* Trans. Walter Kaufmann. New York, NY: Charles Scribner's Sons.

Butler, Judith. 2005. *Giving and Account of Oneself.* New York, NY: Fordham University Press.

Camus, Albert. 1991. *The Myth of Sisyphus and Other Essays.* Trans. Justin O'Brien. New York, NY: Vintage.

Caputo, John D. 2015. *Hoping Against Hope: Confessions of a Postmodern Pilgrim.* Minneapolis, MN: Fortress Press.

Chrétien, Jean-Louis. 2004. *The Call and the Response.* Trans. Anne A. Davenport. New York, NY: Fordham University Press.

Chrétien, Jean-Louis. 2002. *The Unforgettable and the Unhoped For.* Trans. Jeffrey Bloechl. New York, NY: Fordham University Press.

Chrétien, Jean-Louis. 2000. "The Wounded Word: Phenomenology of Prayer." In *Phenomenology and the "Theological Turn: the French Debate* by Dominique Janicaud, Jean-François Courtine,

Jean-Louis Chrétien, Jean-Luc Marion, Michel Henry, and Paul Ricœur. New York: Fordham University Press, pp. 147–175.

Derrida, Jacques. 1995. *The Gift of Death*. Trans. David Wills. Chicago, IL and London: University of Chicago Press.

Descartes, René. 1998. *Discourse on Method and Meditations on First Philosophy*, 4th ed. Trans. Donald A. Cress. Indianapolis, IN and Cambridge: Hackett.

Eggers, Dave. *How We Are Hungry*. 2004. New York, NY: Vintage Books.

Eliot, T.S. "The Love Song of J. Alfred Prufrock." Available at https://www.poetryfoundation.org/poetrymagazine/poems/detail/44212. Accessed December 4, 2022.

Emerson, Ralph Waldo. 1981. "Self-Reliance." In *The Portable Emerson*. Ed. Carl bode in collaboration with Malcolm Cowley. New York, NY: Penguin Books, pp. 138-164.

Frankl, Viktor. 2006. *Man's Search for Meaning*, Trans. Ilse Lasch. Boston, MA: Beacon Press.

Gros, Frédéric. 2015. *A Philosophy of Walking*. Trans. John Howe. London and New York, NY: Verso.

Hadot, Pierre. *Philosophy as a Way of Life: Spiritual Exercises from Socrates to Foucault*. Ed. Arnold I. Davidson. Trans. Michael Chase. Malden, MA and Oxford: Blackwell.

Heidegger, Martin. 2010. *Being and Time*. Trans. Joan Stambaugh, rev. Dennis J. Schmidt. Albany and New York: State University of New York Press.

James, Aaron. 2017. *Surfing with Sartre: An Aquatic Inquiry into a Life of Meaning*. New York, Anchor Books.

James, Aaron. 2012. *Assholes: A Theory*. New York, NY: Anchor Books.

Kaag, John. 2018. *Hiking with Nietzsche: On Becoming Who You Are*. New York, NY: Farrar, Straus, Giroux.

Kierkegaard, Søren. 1996. *Papers and Journals: A Selection*. Trans. Alastair Hannay. London: Penguin Books.

Kierkegaard, Søren. 1992. *Concluding Unscientific Postscript to* Philosophical Fragments, vol. 1. Ed. and trans. Howard V. Hong and Edna H. Hong. Princeton, NJ: Princeton University Press.

Kierkegaard, Søren. 1988. *Stages on Life's Way*. Ed. and trans. Howard V. Hong and Edna H. Hong. Princeton, NJ: Princeton University Press.

Kierkegaard, Søren. 1983. *Fear and Trembling and Repetition*. Ed. and trans. Howard V. Hong and Edna H. Hong. Princeton, NJ: Princeton University Press.

Kierkegaard, Søren. 1948. *Purity of Heart is to Will One Thing*. Trans. Douglas V. Steere. New York, NY: Harper and Row.

Lamott, Anne. 2018. *Almost Everything: Notes on Hope*. New York, NY: Riverhead Books.

Lamott, Anne. 2012. *Help, Thanks, Wow: The Three Essential Prayers*. New York, NY: Riverhead Books.

Lane, Belden C. 2015. *Backpacking with the Saints: Wilderness Hiking as Spiritual Practice*. Oxford: Oxford University Press.

Levinas, Emmanuel. 1987. *Collected Philosophical Papers*. Trans. Alphonso Lingis. Pittsburgh, PA: Duquesne University Press.

Levinas, Emmanuel. 1985. *Ethics and Infinity: Conversations with Philippe Nemo*. Trans. Richard A. Cohen. Pittsburgh, PA: Duquesne University Press.

Levinas, Emmanuel. 1969. *Totality and Infinity: An Essay on Exteriority*. Trans. Alphonso Lingis. Pittsburgh, PA: Duquesne University Press.

Lewis, C.S. 2015. *The Great Divorce*. San Francisco, CA: HarperOne.

Lewis, C.S. 1960. *The Four Loves*. New York, NY: Harcourt Brace & Company, 1960.

Marx, Karl. 1978. "Economic and Philosophic Manuscripts of 1844." In *The Marx-Engels Reader*, 2nd ed. Ed. Robert C. Tucker. New York, NY: W.W. Norton.

May, Todd. 2017. *A Fragile Life: Accepting Our Vulnerability*. Chicago, IL and London: University of Chicago Press.

Minister, Stephen. 2012. *De-Facing the Other: Reason, Ethics, and Politics after Difference*. Milwaukee, WI: Marquette University Press.

Nagel, Thomas. 1979. *Mortal Questions*. Cambridge: Cambridge University Press.

Riggle, Nick. 2022. *This Beauty: A Philosophy of Being Alive*. New York, NY: Basic Books.

Romano, Claude. 2014. *Event and Time*. Trans. Stephen E. Lewis. New York, NY: Fordham University Press.

Romano, Claude. 2009. "Awaiting." In *Phenomenology and Eschatology: Not Yet in the Now*. Ed. Neal DeRoo and John Panteleimon Manoussakis. Trans. Ryan Coyne. Farnham and Burlington: VT: Ashgate, 2009, pp. 35–52.

Sartre, Jean-Paul. 1989. *No Exit and Three Other Plays*. Trans. Stuart Gilbert. New York, NY: Vintage.

Sartre, Jean-Paul. 1985. *Existentialism and Human Emotions*. Trans. Bernard Frechtman and Hazel E. Barnes. Seacaucus, NJ: Carol Publishing Group.

Schilbrack, Kevin. 2014. *Philosophy and the Study of Religions: A Manifesto*. Malden, MA: Wiley-Blackwell.

Seneca. 2018. *How to Die: An Ancient Guide to the End of Life*. Ed. and trans. James S. Romm. Princeton, NJ: Princeton University Press.

Simmons J. Aaron and Eli Simmons. 2023. "Liturgy and Eschatological Hope," in *Philosophies of Liturgy: Philosophical Explorations of Embodied Religious Practice*. Ed. J. Aaron Simmons, Neal DeRoo, and Bruce Ellis Benson.

Simmons, J. Aaron. 2023. "Vagueness and Its Virtues: A Proposal for Renewing Philosophy of Religion." *Philosophy of Religion After "Religion."* Eds. Richard Amesbury and Michael Ch. Rodgers. Tübingen: Mohr Siebeck.

Simmons. J. Aaron. 2017. "Living Joyfully after Losing Social Hope: Kierkegaard and Chrétien on Selfhood and Eschatological Expectation." *Religions* 8, no. 33: 1–15;

Simmons, J. Aaron. 2015. "A Search for the 'Really' Real: Philosophically Approaching the Task of Defining Religion," *Bulletin for the Study of Religion* 44, no.4 (December): 19–26.

Simmons, J. Aaron. 2011. *God and the Other: Ethics and Politics After the Theological Turn*. Bloomington and Indianapolis, IN: Indiana University Press.

Tennyson, Alfred Lord. "Ulysses." In *Poems of Tennyson.* Ed. Jerome H. Buckley. Boston, MA: Houghton Mifflin, pp. 66-67.

Thoreau, Henry David. 2006. "Walking." In *The American Transcendentalists: Essential Writings.* Ed. Lawrence Buell. New York, NY: The Modern Library, pp. 329-335.

Thoreau, Henry David. *Walden and Other Writings.* 1993. New York, NY: Barnes and Noble Classics.

Tolstoy, Leo N. 1912. "The Wisdom of Children." In *Father Sergius, the Wisdom of Children, Miscellaneous Stories.* Ed. Hagberg Wright. New York, NY and Boston, MA: Colonial Press Co., pp. 97-188.

Wallace, David Foster. 2009. *This is Water.* New York, NY: Little, Brown, and Company.

Weil, Simone. 2005. "The Iliad, or The Poem of Force." In *War and the Iliad* by Simone Weil and Rachel Bespaloff. Trans. Mary McCarthy. New York, NY: New York Review Books, pp. 1-38.

Acknowledgements

This book owes so much to so many. A special thanks to everyone who encouraged me to write it for years before I ever wrote the first word.

Inspiration for this book is due to other philosophers who took the risk to do philosophy in the mountains, as it were: Aaron James's *Surfing with Sartre* (2017), Belden C. Lane's *Backpacking with the Saints* (2015), Frédéric Gros's *A Philosophy of Walking* (2015), and John Kaag's *Hiking with Nietzsche* (2018). These books are so influential on my own thinking that I dare not cite them specifically in what follows. Instead, their presence is felt throughout. I am appreciative of their excellence and their example.

I am deeply grateful to Inese Radzins for permission to use the correspondence with David Kangas in Chapter 10.

Chapter 8 (in a very different, and much more technical, version) first appeared in *Art, Desire, and God: Phenomenological Perspectives*, edited by Kevin Grove, Christopher Rios, and Taylor Nutter (Bloomsbury, 2023).

I cannot express deeply enough how thankful I am to Steven Bryant for the use of his mountain cabin. It became my writing retreat and nearly every word of this book was composed there outside Jones Gap State Park while looking over the Blue Ridge Mountains (the rest of the words were largely written at campsites, by rivers, and on mountain balds). I can honestly say that had he not be so generous with his cabin and so supportive with his encouragement that I go there and write, this book would not have been completed.

Thanks also to Nathan Loewen who encouraged me to start riding mountain bikes, Waylon Bigsby who showed me how to do it well, Andrej Suttles for getting me out on the trails more frequently, and Seth Cain for being my constant riding partner ever since. A huge thanks to Waylon also for designing the cover for this book.

I am appreciative to those who have read drafts of chapters and given feedback to me along the way: Amber Bowen, Zach Jolly, Devin Zhang, Josh Patterson, Shannon Duke, John Sanders, and especially Tom Morris, who has provided advice and enthusiasm throughout the process.

Let me also give a big shout out to the Furman University Fly and Fish Club and also the Mountain Bike Interest Group ("Dirt Church"). It has been my joy to help established these clubs and work with the amazing students who are involved in them. A lot of what has gone into these chapters got worked through while out in the woods with my students.

A special thanks to Vanessa and Atticus for their constant inspiration in every area of my life. They give me energy for the climbs and courage for the downhills.

Finally, were it not for my dad, John Simmons, I would never have learned to venture into the woods in order to find myself. For my entire life he has modeled virtue, excellence, how to catch trout, and how still to have a great day when the fish are not striking.

About the Author

J. Aaron Simmons was born near the Hiwassee River in Tennessee, grew up near the beaches of Florida, and now lives in the Carolina mountains. Simmons paid his way through college by working construction and playing drums professionally. He is now a professor of philosophy at Furman University in Greenville, South Carolina and specializes in philosophy of religion, existentialism, and phenomenology. Having published widely, Simmons is the author or editor of numerous books including *God and the Other* (Indiana University Press), *The New Phenomenology* (Bloomsbury), *Christian Philosophy* (Oxford University Press), *Kierkegaard's God and the Good Life* (Indiana University Press), *Philosophies of Liturgy* (Bloomsbury), and *Re-Examining Deconstruction and Determinate Religion* (Duquesne University Press), among others. An award-winning teacher, Simmons's essays have appeared in some of the most distinguished journals in philosophy and religious studies, and he is a widely sought-after public speaker. Simmons is the former President of the Søren Kierkegaard Society (USA), the former President of the South Carolina Society for Philosophy, sits on the Executive Board of the Society for Continental Philosophy and Theology, and has held other professional positions with the Society of Christian Philosophers and The American Academy of Religion. Simmons is actively engaged in public philosophy on his influential YouTube channel, "Philosophy for Where We Find Ourselves," and he has been interviewed for numerous podcasts. An avid mountain biker and trout fisherman, Simmons thinks philosophy is always relevant to life. He has been married to his wife, Vanessa for 22 years and they have a thirteen-year-old son, Atticus, who loves parkour, drums, and skateboarding.

You can find out more about Aaron, and get signed up for his monthly newsletter, at his website: https://jaaronsimmons.com/